Different Drummers
They Did What They Wanted

Antoinette May

LES FEMMES
Millbrae, California

For Clara Trusel—my mother

Also By Antoinette May
Haunted Ladies

10-85

Copyright © 1976 by Antoinette May

Published by LES FEMMES
231 Adrian Road
Millbrae, California 94030

First Printing, July 1976
Made in the United States of America

Library of Congress Cataloging in Publication Data

May, Antoinette.
  Different drummers.

  1. Women—Biography. I. Title.
CT3234.M37   920.72   76-11373
ISBN 0-89087-907-9

  2 3 4 5 6 7 8 - 81 80 79 78 77

Bookstore
gift

Contents

*If a man does not keep pace with his companions,
perhaps it is because he hears a different drummer.
Let him step to the music which he hears,
however measured or far away.*

Henry David Thoreau

Introduction

For some women there are no halfway measures in life—
there is only a raw passion of one sort or another. As though
possessed by some inner demon, they must play out their
lives like shooting stars against the dark gray sky of convention.

While dazzling or defying the world about them, they
manage to exert a very real fascination. Decades later it still
remains.

A few such individuals—at much cost to themselves—
made the world a more exciting place while they lived and
departed leaving a heritage of new options. We, the women
of today, are their heirs—only now beginning to fully enjoy
the legacy bequeathed us.

Two choices have traditionally existed for women: to be
good or to be *bad*.

To be a "Good Woman" has meant to be a wife/mother, a
tower of strength and unquestioning devotion, a nonin-
dividual expected to subordinate her own drives or desires to
the whims of her husband or the needs of her children. She
is the Mother-of-the-Year who scrubs floors to send eighteen
children through college. The possibility that, given control
over her own life, she might have not had children and gone
to college herself seemed unthinkable—to others. It is
enough that she experienced the glory of sacrifice.

The "Bad Woman" is merely the same support system
functioning in party clothes. The beautiful but damned
femme fatal, personified in real life by Zelda Fitzgerald and
perpetuated in literature by such ill-fated butterflies as Nana

1

and Camille, is a glittering sacrifice to the still present myth that it is an end in itself to please and amuse a man.

In his novel, *Tender is the Night*, F. Scott Fitzgerald wrote of Nicole Diver (a character patterned after Zelda) and two other women that he admired: "They were all happy to exist in a man's world—they preserved their individuality through men and not by opposition to them. They would all three have made alternatively good courtesans or good wives not by the accident of birth but through the greater accident of finding their man or not finding him."

How little he knew or understood his own multifaceted wife, a woman whose many talents had been subordinated to his greater ego, leaving merely a tragic charade of trivial frivolity.

The six women selected for this collective biography rejected both of these roles. They refused to be defined by the demands or expectations of husbands, lovers or children. It was not enough merely to hear the faint tattoo of a different drummer. Each was determined to *own* the drum.

All insisted upon living their own lives, being their own women, following their own paths—even when those uncharted courses came into open conflict with the desires of those closest and dearest to them.

Better a bitch than a victim, each seems to have decided and never wavered from her choice. But theirs was not the idle, senseless machinations of the compulsive shrew, who—realizing the emptiness of her existence, but lacking the initiative and intelligence to change it—can do nothing beyond destroy the happiness of those around her. Here, instead, is a calculated bitchiness—the consumate, superb determination to fight against and even overcome the cruelty of circumstance.

The goals of these women—politics, spiritualism, dancing, acting, singing, and flying—were highly selective, as were their means of achievement against every kind of opposition.

By never doubting the validity of such ambitions or her own ultimate ability to attain them, each woman advanced to the position that she desired. Many others have been equally gifted, but few were—or are—as dedicated to the fulfillment of those gifts as the women whose lives will be revealed in the upcoming pages of this book.

What qualities link such divergent personalities as Victoria Woodhull, Helena Blavatsky, Isadora Duncan, Ernestine Schumann-Heink, Sarah Bernhardt, and Amelia Earhart?

Originality. Singlemindedness. Great courage. Supreme self-confidence and an equal amount of self-discipline.

Each was a woman who enjoyed being a woman but insisted upon playing the game of life by making men's rules work for them—despite the considerable penalties involved. Each might have lightened the load through compromise and conciliation, but steadfastly refused to do so. And each during the course of an arduous and tempestuous life could have paused to enjoy hard won ease and comfort; but totally disregarded the possibility, choosing to remain an activist to the very end.

What to do and what to leave undone without repining? Which things matter forever? These six great heroines of the social revolution were unique in that they knew the answers to the existential questions that ultimately plague us all. Each, having solved the riddle of her own existence, could live freely and fully without compromise.

Emerging from a tawdry youth in the backwoods of Ohio, Victoria Woodhull could have been a great hostess and courtesan, enjoying all the material benefits that a hypocritical Victorian society could offer a beautiful and audacious woman.

Instead, she chose to revolutionize that society. "Men were created for *our* pleasure," she confided to the women of the world, foreshadowing the myriad right to orgasm articles popular today. By insisting that sex be recognized as a pleasant fact of life for the godly as well as the ungodly, she changed the thinking of her entire generation—and with it the thinking and behavior patterns of generations to come.

Another who subordinated romantic and familial ties to the conquest of the world of ideas was Helena Blavatsky who, at seventeen, abandoned a life of feudal luxury in Czarist Russia to explore the world. Twenty-five years later—at a time when women traveling alone were not yet allowed to stay in better hotels—she had explored the jungles of Africa and India and climbed the Andes Mountains. At voodoo rites in the West Indies, from Tibetan monks, Indian shamans, African witch doctors, Hindu holy men, and Persian sorcerers, she learned strange secrets. These she determined to share with the world.

Blavatsky was the consumate pushy broad, loud-mouthed, foul-mouthed and corpulent—she was abhorred by some and adored by others. Like Moses, Christ, Buddha, and Mohammed before her, she claimed miracles and divine inspiration. As a high priestess, she was much maligned; but, as a result of her efforts, occult mysticism and the doctrine of reincarnation were introduced to the western world.

Isadora Duncan and Sarah Bernhardt both determined to become the top artist in their respective fields. Each of them realized very early that such ambition was incompatible with marriage or any long term commitment. Unlike many of their contemporaries, the stage meant far more than just a showcase for their natural endowments—they were dedicated to the perfection of their art. There simply was no time for marital demands. The obvious solution for women of their careless confidence was a series of affairs but if there was keeping to be done, both would prefer to be the keeper rather than the kept. Others gasped with amazement as a parade of dazzling dramas was played out in bold, black headlines. Why should any woman marry if it didn't suit her personal style, was the issue raised by example. More than fifty years later the question is still hotly debated.

Ernestine Schumann-Heink and Amelia Earhart were notable exceptions to the others who generally adhered to the adage, "she travels fastest who travels alone." Ernestine, lacking the authority of beauty, succumbed to the blandishments of a young clerk who flattered her lonely heart. The marriage that followed their elopement was a disaster.

Despite the birth of many children, which invariably materialized in those pre-pill times, it never occurred to Ernestine to abandon her career. She sang just hours before the birth of one baby and literally nursed them all between arias. There were two more marriages and even more children. Ernestine's American debut was made one month before the birth of her seventh child; there were twenty curtain calls. The greatest female singer of her time, Ernestine Schumann-Heink disproves forever the anti-feminist catchphrase: anatomy is destiny. Destiny was something she would decide for herself, a goal seen very clearly. She would be a star. The children would simply have to adjust to her needs—not she to theirs. They adjusted.

On the subject of babies, Amelia Earhart's attitude was that children were nice for others, but not for herself. It "took too long to make a baby," she complained. "There were too many exciting things to be done in an airplane."

This same unwillingness to forego any of the excitement implicit in her life had kept Amelia from marrying until well into her thirties. There had been numerous proposals, for the pioneer aviator was considered one of the most exciting and attractive women in the entire world; but she remained coolly self-sufficient, explaining: "I can think of lots of things worse than never getting married. One of the worst is being married to a man who tied you down." With this grim possibility in mind, Amelia wrote her own marriage contract nearly fifty years ago. The marriage—ended by her tragic disappearance—appears to have been a happy one, largely because of adherence to a contract guaranteeing Amelia *all* the open space her restless soul required.

Surveying these "different drummers" over a span of years, one recognizes immediately that each achieved success as she, herself, defined it. Did that hard earned success bring happiness? One would assume so, since only death itself could stop them from continuing to pursue lifelong goals. Because these courageous individualists were ridiculed, ostracized and condemned but continued on their way unbroken, we are free today to enjoy a plentitude of possibilities and a growing measure of tolerance.

For all of the women there were periods of intense emotional isolation. Yet surely these exist in every life—albeit conventional. One can only study the alternatives to our choices. Nobody gets security *and* adventure, safety *and* excitement, contentment *and* variety. Not at one time anyway, rarely in one lifetime.

Here are six women who are unique in that they knew what they wanted—and got it. They heard a far different

drummer than that regulating the tread of their more sub-
servient and compliant sisters and went in search of it. They
dared to be different and were.

Antoinette May
Palo Alto, California   May 1976

1

Victoria Woodhull

The Angry Siren Who Destroyed a Saint

"How dared she—is she witch or woman?" outraged society speculated in 1872 when Victoria Woodhull, a notorious, seductive seer declared herself a candidate for the presidency of the United States. Free love was the major plank in her presidential platform. She also advocated spiritualism, world government, a universal language, birth control, easier divorces, abolition of the death penalty, better public housing, excess profit taxes, and shorter skirts. In an age of hypocrisy, such views could not go unchallenged.

No woman before or since dared so much and defied so many. Whether it was the dark attraction of mysticism or the strident cry of sexual equality, Victoria possessed the courage to act on her convictions and challenge every convention of her time.

In January of the previous year she had addressed the United States Congress—the first woman to do so. Fragile, feminine with a dainty rose pinned to her stylish gown, Victoria Woodhull dispelled masculine visions of fearsome feminists fighting for woman's suffrage. Once charmed into listening the politicians ultimately applauded her logic. "While others argued the equality of women, I proved it by successfully engaging in business," she reminded her audience. She then went on to urge that the right to vote should no more be denied to women than it had been to blacks. "A race comprises *all* people, male and female," she reasoned. The recent removal of the race barrier with the ratification of the Fifteenth Amendment made the continued disenfranchisement of women all the more absurd.

Her Congressional appearance was a milestone for the woman's movement and a personal triumph for Woodhull. Liberated, non-conforming, scandalous, this great heroine of the social revolution was determined to rise above her tawdry origins. She had been born to a family distinguished only by its combined efforts to avoid law, order and respectability. The date was September 23, 1838. The place was Homer, Ohio, still a rough, lawless frontier. Victoria's father, a former stableman called "Buck" Claflin, was a promoter as unlucky in his schemes as he was unscrupulous. Card shark, land dealer, he was involved in a wide ranging assortment of illegal activities including patent medicines—for which he was run out of more than one town. Her mother Roxanna—highly imaginative, but a totally illiterate former maid—had a noisy penchant for backyard revival meetings and family feuding.

Victoria believed herself to have been conceived during one of the many frenzied Methodist revival meetings her parents attended. This she felt marked her "from the womb with preternatural excitement."

Victoria's early years were spent moving from one Ohio town to another just one step ahead of the law. Emotional, unreliable, sometimes alarming, the Claflins fought with everyone including each other.

In contrast, Victoria, their fifth child, was quiet and self-contained. She quickly found release from the harsh realities of her squalid existence and was given to going into trances. She is said to have exhibited powers of clairvoyance as a very young child. Years later she told of falling into a swoon at the age of three after the death of a neighbor. The spirit of a dead little friend carried her off to another world where she saw "beautiful flowers and all sorts of wonderful sights."

A contemporary biographer relates, "In her tenth year, one day while sitting by the side of a cradle rocking a sick babe to sleep, she says that two angels came, and gently pushing her away, began to fan the sick child with their white hands, until its face grew fresh and rosy. Her mother suddenly entered the chamber, and beheld in amazement the little nurse lying in a trance on the floor, her face turned toward the ceiling and the pining babe apparently in the bloom of health."

In later life Victoria recalled playing as a child with the spirits of her two baby sisters who had died before her birth. (She preferred their company to that of her raucous live siblings.) But the most dramatic spirit visitor was a noble appearing man in a white tunic. "You will know wealth and fame one day," he promised. "You will live in a mansion in a city surrounded by ships and you will become a leader of your people."

Such encouragement may have provided inspiration as well as solace. Surely something set Victoria apart from the others in her family. The lone white lamb in the flock never acquired the reportedly piercing whine of her mother or the bold manners of her older sisters. There was no "lady" in her life to emulate and almost no formal education, but somehow Victoria developed taste, elegance and a soft-spoken yet compelling personality that would ultimately command the respect of the nation's intelligentsia.

When Victoria was thirteen, word was received that her

sister, Tennessee—the tenth and last Claflin child who had
been farmed out as an infant to relatives in Pennsylvania—
was behav ng "strangely." Tennessee Celeste, who would
one day be known across the country as the flamboyant
"Tennie C.," was frightening her playmates by reading their
minds. The six-year-old had amazed a farmer by revealing
the whereabouts of his lost calf. The farmer was delighted
but others were alarmed when the child then went on to
accurately predict a seminary fire. An investigation proved
the girl's innocence but could not explain away her "queer-
ness."

The Claflins welcomed back their youngest with open
arms. They were all a bit queer, nothing different about her.
Besides Buck had plans for his two pretty little clairvoyants.

Soon Victoria and Tennie were supporting the whole family by conducting seances, tipping tables, revealing mystic
truths and inducing miraculous cures. Neighbors frequently
complained about the strange noises and wild shrieks that
emanated from the boardinghouse parlor while the girls
were communing with the spirits, but Buck was an expert at
finding new locations in a hurry and they were able to keep
moving.

The girls each viewed the experience differently. Tennie
treated the spirits as lightly as she treated everything else,
but Victoria took her powers seriously. Like many clairvoyants, Victoria may have felt the occasional need to urge
on the reluctant spirits with a few tricks of her own. She had
a reputation to maintain and a family to feed. A fickle public
would not allow for off days—nor would Buck Claflin. But
Victoria was firm in her belief in these incorporeal entities
themselves and in her own ability to summon them.
Throughout her long and colorful life, Victoria remained totally committed to belief in her own mystical powers.

For a time the girls were happy with the attention and the
regular diet their performances brought. They were also
pleased with one another. Victoria's gravity was lightened
by the gaiety of Tennie who was the first and the most loyal
of her many admirers.

Marriage to Dr. Canning Woodhull, a young physician her
father brought home, temporarily broke up the sister act.
Whatever Victoria may have thought of the man, Buck per-

ceived him as a great catch. It was another of Buck Claflin's many mistakes.

Three days after the marriage, the fifteen-year-old bride was temporarily deserted by her husband who spent the night at a house of prostitution. As a later lover and biographer, Theodore Tilton, delicately described it: "She learned to her dismay that Woodhull was habitually unchaste and given to long fits of intoxication. Fifteen months later "while living in a little, low frame house in Chicago, in the dead of winter, with icicles clinging to her bedpost, and attended only by her drunken husband, she brought forth in almost mortal agony her first born child." To add to Victoria's despair, the child, Byron, was mentally retarded.

Woodhull's drunken "fits" increased, his medical practice declined as they continually moved about the country. Soon the teenage bride and mother had become the breadwinner of the family, working as a cigar girl, seamstress and entertainer in dance halls. While dancing in a Barbary Coast saloon, Victoria was spotted by Anna Cogswell, a popular San Francisco actress, who gave her a small part to play. Within six weeks she was earning $52 a week, an attractive sum in those days.

Mystical forces put a sudden end to this budding career. Recounting the experience a few years later to the editor of the *Brooklyn Independent*, Victoria remembered that she was performing in the ballroom scene of *The Corsican Brothers* clad in a pink silk dress and slippers. Suddenly a spirit voice commanded: "Victoria, come home!" Lapsing into a deep trance, Victoria beheld Tennessee wearing a striped calico frock beckoning her. "The apparition was not to be denied." she explained.

The show went on without Victoria. Without bothering to change her dress, she rushed to her hotel. Within hours, Victoria, her husband and Byron were on board a steamer bound for the East Coast. Reaching land, they journeyed immediately to Columbus, Ohio where the spirits had revealed that Tennessee would be waiting.

Once reunited, the sisters were back in business. Just a few of their much publicized feats included catching bank robbers with the aid of tattling spirits and curing the lame and the deaf through divine intervention.

It was during this period that a second child was born to Victoria under circumstances almost as harrowing as her first confinement. The baby, a girl, would exhibit none of the *joie de vivre* that characterized the Claflin clan but was mentally sound. (Perhaps all her energies were exhausted in attempting to live up to the name Zulu Maude.)

In 1866, eighteen years had passed since the noble spirit's strange prophesy that had dominated Victoria's childhood. Though her life was no longer governed by the vicissitudes of Buck Claflin's deals, the vagabond existence of an itinerant clairvoyant was a far cry from the grandiose predictions that had helped to form her character. Suddenly a prophesy of her own changed everything. "I see our futures linked," she informed Colonel James Blood, a handsome pillar of St. Louis society who had sought her services as a spiritualist. "Our destinies are bound together by the ties of marriage."

Believing themselves to be instantly betrothed by "the powers of the air," Victoria and Blood were ecstatic. Colonel Blood abandoned his wife and family and his position as city auditor to take off alone with Victoria in a covered wagon through the Ozarks. Working as an advance man, he publicized the impending arrival of a "great seeress" who could read the past and future while advising on the spiritual, physical and emotional aspects of the present.

The trip was a romantic success as well as a financial one. Between engagements there was ample opportunity for the lovers to explore secluded mountain lanes. Stopping along the way, they made love beside rushing streams or amidst groves of sighing pines. Both returned convinced that they belonged together and that the key to human happiness lay in honest, unrestrained sexuality. The sharing of this concept with a seemingly ungrateful world became a lifelong crusade for Victoria.

Later as her free love doctrine crystallized, she would proclaim: "The love that I cannot command is not mine; let me not disturb myself about it, nor attempt to filch it from its rightful owners. . . . Rather let me leave my doors and windows open, intent only on living as nobly that the best cannot fail to be drawn to me by irresistible attraction." For those who lost at love she would advise: "Withdraw lov-

ingly, but completely, all claim and all complaint as an injured or deserted husband or wife. Be kind to and sympathe-
tic with the new attraction, rather than waspish or indignant."

For the moment there were Mrs. Blood and Canning
Woodhull to be dealt with on a more personal level. Awak-
ening briefly from a drunken stupor, Woodhull accepted Victoria's departure docilely. Mrs. Blood's withdrawal was anything but loving. It took the entire proceeds from their
psychic expedition to persuade her to obtain a divorce.

After their marriage St. Louis seemed a small place to con-
tain them all. Then one day while meditating, Victoria was
visited again by the spirit benefactor of her childhood who
had promised wealth, fame and leadership. "Go," he said,
"to New York City. Go to 17 Great Jones Street. There you
will find a house ready and waiting for you and yours." A
vision of a house and then of its interior floated momentarily
beside the spirit form.

"Who are you?" Victoria gasped.

The ghostly specter stretched forth a hand. With one
finger, he traced eleven letters on the table before her. The
letters began to grow brighter and brighter until they illumi-
nated the room. They spelled the name, *Demosthenes.* How
the unlettered Victoria managed to recognize the name of the
greatest orator of ancient Greece is perhaps another miracle,
but she did recognize it and followed the advice without
question.

Victoria, Colonel Blood, Zulu Maude and Byron, joined by
Tennie, went immediately to New York. Proceeding to the
address, they found a house exactly as Victoria had envisioned it. Inside, on a parlor table, she discovered a book.
Stamped in gold on its cover was the title, *The Orations of
Demosthenes.* She felt, she wrote later, "a blood-chilling astonishment" at this confirmation of her spirit guide's identity. It did indeed seem that the Athenian speaker (who had
taken his life by biting off a portion of a poison pen after
leading an abortive revolt against tyranny) had returned to
earth to inspire another silver tongued orator in the person
of Victoria Woodhull. This time the target was to be hypocrisy and puritanical convention.

The house was vacant and available. It was a comfortable brownstone large enough to accommodate the five of them and the rest of the Claflin clan—Buck, Roxanna, sisters, brothers, in-laws, nieces and nephews—who soon followed.

Victoria and Tennie burst upon the New York scene with the force of twin typhoons. Tennie was bewitchingly pretty, light-hearted, loving with a handy talent for flattery. She was a great favorite with newspaper men and New York dandies who affectionately teased her with the song, "Oh, that ten-ten-Tennessee!"

Victoria was even more beautiful, and possessed the intelligence to utilize Tennie's sex appeal and her own for more than just monetary profit. At thirty-one, she had acquired an easy elegance. Her clothes were chic and understated, calling attention subtly to her extraordinary features—curly auburn hair, daringly bobbed, high cheekbones and flawless skin. She was a colorful conversationalist "apt to call things by their right names, and guiltless of prudery or sham modesty." She could listen as well, gazing intently into the eyes of her companion.

Victoria must have listened very carefully, absorbing thoughts as well as words from the prominent people who frequented her fashionable salon. Victoria credited Demosthenes for her ability and sudden success, but it may be she was a remarkably quick study. Whichever—a country girl with only three years of formal education was soon lecturing on world government seventy-five years before the birth of the United Nations.

She also spoke easily and well on finance and pointed out political graft far in advance of Theodore Roosevelt, who thirty-four years later coined the word "muckracker." In 1870 she urged sex education, insisting that "if our houses of prostitution were searched and their inmates questioned, none would be found whose mother had the good sense to teach them the objects and functions of their sexual systems."

Many skeptics believed that Victoria's prepared material was dictated by a livelier, more mortal personage than Demosthenes—Colonel Blood, perhaps—yet the fact remained that she could speak extemporaneously with equal eloquence. Victoria's grasp of and enthusiasm for grand concepts could not be challenged by even the most cynical. The two Claflin sisters between them would soon acquire not only vast amounts of cash but tremendous influence, creating a social force of sufficient potency to affect the course of United States history.

Susan B. Anthony and Elizabeth Cady Stanton, the suffrage greats, were among Victoria's staunch admirers. Of her the latter once enthusiastically gushed: "The nature that can pass through all phases of social degradation, vice, crime, poverty, and temptation in all its forms and yet maintain a dignity and purity of character through it all, gives unmistakable proof of its high origin, its divinity."

Horace Greeley—a man who sometimes ran editorials favoring communism, but was not radical enough to support women's rights—even had a few nice things to say about her. For him, Victoria was "a spirit to respect, perhaps to fear for she had the courage of her opinions."

Another admirer was Cornelius Vanderbilt, who supplemented moral support with economic aid. Known as the Commodore, this eccentric but powerful founder of the Vanderbilt fortune, was eager to receive financial guidance from his dead friend, Jim Fiske. Victoria and Tennessee were delighted to assist. It is said that Victoria once materialized the spirit of Vanderbilt's dead wife, Sophia, but the seventy-six-year-old Commodore rejected the apparition; "business before pleasure," he insisted. "Let me speak to Jim."

If Fiske's stock market tips relayed through Victoria or Tennie occasionally conflicted with his own shrewd judgment, the Commodore was understanding. Jim had always had his off moments, he philosophized. Besides he was even more interested in the massage parlor aspect of the sisters' operation. So aroused was Vanderbilt that he proposed to Tennie—his "Little Sparrow"—but she gently refused him. Not at all rebuffed, he agreed to set the sisters up as stockbrokers; their brokerage house was the first in Wall Street history to be run by women.

Undoubtedly Vanderbilt augmented their spiritual counsel with a little earthly information of his own for the brokerage firm was highly successful. Subtle credit went to Tennie's "Old Boy" in the form of a portrait in the foyer of their office. Beneath Vanderbilt's picture was the inscription, *Simply to thy cross I cling.* It was a hefty cross, for Vanderbilt was the richest American of his time. The sisters, who hated hypocrisy above all else, clearly were hiding nothing.

The press labeled Victoria and Tennie C., "Queens of Finance," "Bewitching Brokers" and "Fascinating Financeers," as they graciously granted dozens of interviews. Each had a gold pencil tucked behind a pretty ear and wore a smart black broadcloth suit severely tailored to enhance a voluptuous figure. Victoria was direct and to the point, "All this talk about women's rights is moonshine," she told a reporter. "Women have every right. All they need to do is exercise them."

Effervescent Tennie was equally vocal. "I think a woman is just as capable of making a living as a man and I have seen men so vain of their personal appearance and so effeminate that I should be sorry to compare my intelligence to theirs."

The *New York Herald* which had announced the brokerage opening with the condescending greeting, "Vive la frou frou," had now changed its tune. A reporter commented of Victoria and Tennie that "their extraordinary coolness and self-possession, and evident knowledge of the difficult role they have undertaken, is far more remarkable than their personal beauty and graces of manner, and these are considerable."

In three years Woodhull, Claflin & Co. amassed $75,000 in profits. Victoria was jubilant. She didn't need Demosthenes to prompt her announcement that "women's ability to earn money is a better protection against the tyranny and brutality of men than her ability to vote." The Claflin clan moved from 17 Great Jones Street to a more fashionable Murray Hill address. Victoria commented that it took $25,000 a month to keep them all. The menage now included Victoria, Tennie, their parents, three sisters—Margaret Ann with her four children, Polly with her husband and two children and Utica with her bottle. The latter sister tried to conceal her mounting envy of Victoria by frequent alcoholic binges that added further to the Claflin notoriety. In addition to Zulu Maude,

Byron and Colonel Blood there was also Stephen Pearl Andrews, a famous radical philosopher who had come for a
weekend and remained for several years sharing the fortunes of the flamboyant family.

The most controversial resident was Canning Woodhull
who had arrived one morning totally destitute. He was in the
last stages of alcoholism, addicted now to morphine as well.
Victoria took him in and provided care for the ailing man
until his death a few years later. Society was scandalized by
the idea of two "husbands" under one roof but Victoria was
unconcerned. She bore Woodhull no malice. To deny him
sanctuary in time of need to avoid gossip would have been
hypocrisy. Besides the two men were the most amiable
members of the extended family.

There were far more important issues for Victoria. Having
acquired wealth, she was ready to move on to power. In 1870
the sisters commenced publication of *Woodhull & Claflin's
Weekly*, a journal dedicated to equal rights for women and a
single moral standard for all. The *Weekly*'s motto was "Prog-
ress! Free Thought! Untrammeled Lives!" It matched Victoria's philosophy perfectly. "The paper," she assured her
reading public, "would be devoted to the vital interests of
the people."

And indeed it was. Victoria plunged right in with frank
advice on birth control. Her journal was the first newspaper
to print the Communist Manifesto in English and to advocate
compulsory classes in physiology for women. When she exposed Wall Street swindles and police shakedown raids on
whorehouses, the circulation soared to undreamed of
heights. Jealously, the *New York Tribune* accused the Weekly
of favoring prostitution, citing the shakedown exposes. But,
while moralizing on the editorial page, the Tribune continued to run advertisements for whorehouses—something
the *Weekly* never allowed.

There were rumors that Colonel Blood and Stephen Pearl
Andrews were the true brains behind the *Weekly*, but Victoria
was quick to set the record straight. "The words fell from my
unconscious lips," the clairvoyant explained; they were dictated by Demosthenes. Colonel Blood was merely the
stenographer who jotted them down. Whatever the source,

the results were sensational. From coast to coast Victorian society gulped when the journal exposed churches that held mortgages on houses of prostitution and choked when it asserted that "the highest order of humanity results from a sexual relations in which love is the only element present."

When not shocking the nation on a grand scale, the sisters found other means of challenging the Establishment. It was not enough to preach equality, they eagerly practiced it. One evening the twosome sauntered into Delmonico's and requested dinner. "You know I can't serve women without male escorts," Charles Delmonico remonstrated. Tennie obligingly dashed out and returned with a coachman. Their party was observed laughing throughout a many course dinner while some diners departed in outrage. Another evening when Victoria was barred from attending the theater without a male escort, she agreeably complied by spontaneously inviting a hall porter to join her in the balcony.

Victoria made headlines across the nation in the course of a lecture she gave several months after her famous congressional address.

"Are you a free lover?" someone called out to her.

"Yes, I'm a free lover," she answered proudly. "I have an inalienable, constitutional and natural right to love whom I may, to love as long or as short a period as I can, to change that love every day if I please!" Free love, she insisted, was better than sex without love even in a union sanctified by marriage.

Stunned by this onslaught of major and minor challenges, staid society gasped once again when Victoria announced her plans to run for president. While the more orthodox feminists prayerfully debated, never quite agreeing on a course of action, Victoria plunged in. She was eager to act. "Why not?" the presidential hopeful demanded to know. "I have already done more for women's rights by demanding them than all the diatribes of paper and platform speeches will do in ten years." (*Or would do in fifty more.*)

Victoria claimed spiritual encouragement in the campaign against Ulysses S. Grant and Horace Greeley from her faithful mentor, Demosthenes. Among her earthly backers was Theodore Tilton, a newspaper editor with great influence.

Their affair was an open one, apparently condoned by Colonel Blood who spent his evenings nursing Canning Woodhull.

Tilton eagerly took on the role of biographer of "the Joan of Arc of the woman's movement." He saw many parallels between the two. For one thing both of them heard voices. His enthusiastic biography included a lengthy account of Victoria's occult experiences. As a result, the National Association of Spiritualists invited her to speak at their national convention in Troy, New York. The cheering throng was so captivated that they unanimously elected Victoria president of their organization. "It was," she recorded in her journal, "the chief honor of my life."

There were other honors as well. At the National Suffrage Association convention, Victoria appeared on the platform flanked by Susan B. Anthony and Elizabeth Cady Stanton who risked their reputations in a gesture of loyalty. Victoria had given them the basis of their suffrage argument in her congressional address. At a time when the more conservative members of their organization were demanding that the controversial Victoria be removed from the society's rolls, the two insisted that she be allowed to address the convention.

Despite what must certainly have been a natural desire for acceptance, Victoria did not attempt to conform to the majority. Instead, she discussed the inflammatory subject of spiritualism—assuring the audience that plans were being formed in the next world for a better world on earth. Such was the strength of Victoria's personal magnetism and the force of her sincerity that the women forgot their hostility, rose to their feet and applauded wildly. It was another Woodhull triumph.

Unfortunately Victoria's personal popularity, congressional acclaim and material success—contrasted with her scandalous notoriety—was viewed as a moral outrage by another pair of sisters, Catherine Beecher and Harriet Beecher Stowe. Catherine was the most violent anti-suffragist of her day. Harriet had been credited by Lincoln as precipitating the Civil War with her incendiary novel, *Uncle Tom's Cabin*.

At Catherine's urging, Harriet undertook to satirize what she termed "the She Devil and her vile immorality" in the *Christian Union*. As the weeks passed with each succeeding chapter of the continuing novel, *My Wife and I*, the unpleasant character of Audacia Dangyereyes became more firmly identifiable as Victoria.

Adding real injury to insult, the Beecher sisters applied pressure on a series of landlords to evict the Claflins. The huge family was hounded from one home to another while Victoria and Tennie attempted to run their newspaper and brokerage firm and Victoria to continue her campaign as presidential candidate for the Equal Rights Party which has formed around her.

"Remember, Victoria Woodhull, that I shall strike you dead," Catherine warned at their one unfortunate confrontation. Undaunted, Victoria replied, "Strike as much and as hard as you please, only don't do it in the dark so that I cannot know who is my enemy." Knowing full well who the enemy was, Victoria angrily retaliated at last by unleashing against the Beechers one of the great social scandals in American history. She intended it to "burst like a bombshell into the ranks of the moralistic camp" and that's exactly what happened.

The Reverend Dr. Henry Ward Beecher—brother of the hostile sisters—was a national symbol of piety. He was also a member of a large and prominent family venerated by the country in much the same way that the Kennedys were during the 1960's. As minister of the commercially successful Plymouth Church, he was considered valuable property by the real estate syndicate that owned the church and drew heavily from its collections. At the peak of his evangelical career, Beecher had been commissioned by a leading publishing company to write a biography of Jesus. Now, just as *The Life of Jesus* was to hit the stands, a huge publicity campaign had been launched to further deify the author.

"I am a woman of destiny," Victoria was fond of saying. She was also a woman totally incapable of staying out of trouble. In threatening to reveal the extra-marital affair of this spiritual superstar with a married Sunday School teacher, Victoria was challenging big business as well as religionists.

"I want your assistance," Victoria wrote Dr. Beecher. "I have been submitted to persecution just so long as I can endure. My business, my projects, in fact everything for which I live, suffers from it, and it must cease. Will you lend me your aid in this?" The preacher claimed later that he did not reply to this "whining letter." In reality, he went to Victoria and literally knelt before her, pleading that she not reveal the scandal that had become an open secret among his family and close associates.

Convinced of her rights, Victoria was implacable. "You're doing secretly what you publicly denounce me for doing," she accused him. "Call off your sisters or the whole world will know what a hypocrite you are." He could not; Beecher was a power in the pulpit but compared to two holy terrors like his sisters, Catherine and Harriet, he was totally ineffectual. His sensational exposure and the ensuing furor that would divide the entire country were inevitable.

There is no question that the charge was true. The unfortunate woman in the affair—later described by a romantic journalist as having "lips full, warm and suggesting robustness of modest passion"—was the wife of Victoria's intimate friend, Theodore Tilton! He had confided everything to her.

On September 11, 1872, in spite of the governor of Massachusett's ban on her public appearance in that state, Victoria spoke before the National Spiritualists' Association convention in Boston. "Suddenly I was seized by one of those overwhelming gusts of inspiration which sometimes come upon me from I know not where—I was taken out of myself," she later explained. Impulsively flinging aside her notes, Victoria preceded to relate in graphic detail everything she knew about the torrid romance between the shepherd of the Plymouth Church and his amorous lamb. She was also quick to point out that the acquiescent Lib Tilton was not the only member of the minister's sexual preserve.

"He preaches every Sunday to dozens of his mistresses, who are members of his church, sitting in their pews, robed in silks and satins and high respectability." Victoria hastened to explain that she was making the disclosure not because she blamed Beecher for his indiscretions, for she herself believed in absolute social and sexual freedom. Her purpose was to force this "man of God"—and all other hypocrites—to acknowledge their own humanity.

The audience was electrified by the disclosure. Sitting at first in stunned silence they waited as if for a Godly thunderbolt to strike Victoria dead. Eventually there came instead a roar of applause. Victoria was unanimously re-elected president of the association. The spiritualists took her unchallenged daring as an omen that all hypocrisy would ultimately be stripped away leaving a clear path open for the better society envisioned for earth by the spirit world.

Despite the enthusiasm of the spiritualists, a curtain of silence obscured the episode from the outside world. Newspapers chose to note that Victoria's speech had been "obnoxious." A famous clergyman had been slandered, a few noted; but none dared say who or in what way. It remained for Victoria to finish the job. "They tell me that I used some naughty words upon occasion," she admitted to her friends, "but all I know is that if I swore I did not swear profanely, and some said with tears streaming from their eyes, that I swore divinely." Victoria was determined to be known as an honest oracle—not a slanderer. She would "relate in formal terms, for the whole world, the simple facts of the case."

On November 2, 1872, the facts were presented in *Woodhull & Claflin's Weekly,* the only paper that would print them. Victoria was tolerant of Beecher's needs. She compassionately cited his "demanding physical nature," and his "immense physical potency." She conceded that the "passional starvation" occasioned by the terrible restrictions upon a minister's life were a "horrid cruelty." Nevertheless, the truth must be told, she insisted. "It is the paradox of my position that, believing in the right of privacy and in the perfect right of Mr. Beecher socially, morally and divinely to have sought the embraces of Mrs. Tilton, or any other woman or women whom he loved and who loved him, I still invade the most secret and sacred affairs of his life, and expose him. . . . What I do is for a purpose," she explained. "The social world is in the very agony of its new birth. Somebody must be hurled forward into the gap."

Hoping to avert this fate, Beecher rushed from newsstand to newsstand in an effort to buy every available copy. It was an impossible task. The first-run was 100,000 copies. These sold at first for fifty cents and finally for $2.50 while additional press runs were hurriedly cranked out. Owners of papers rented them to friends for a dollar a day and some finally paid as much as forty dollars for a single copy.

It was a heady moment for Victoria but soon the ranks of the righteous closed and it was she who was thrown into the gap. Anthony Comstock, a self-styled guardian of morality who made a lively and lucrative living from reading and condemning what he considered to be pornographic literature, eagerly secured a warrant for the arrest of Victoria and her associates on the charge of sending obscene literature through the mails. He was backed by the Young Men's Christian Association. Victoria and Tennessee were arrested and General Noah Davis, the United States District Attorney, asked $10,000 bail for each of them. In attempting to justify the excessive amount, he said: "Not only have the defendants, by circulating an obscene publication through the mails, committed an offense against the law, but they have been guilty of a most abominable and unjust charge against one of the purest and best citizens of this State, or in the United States, and they have, as far as possible, aggravated the offense by an atrocious, malicious, gross and untrue libel upon the character of the gentleman whom the whole country reveres and whose character it is well worth the while of the Government of the United States to vindicate." The name of this pure and great character was not disclosed. United States Commissioner Osborn agreed: "An example is needed and we propose to make one of these women." Prohibitive bail was finally set at $8,000 for each defendant.

The sisters were then incarcerated in an eight-by-four-foot cell. Police were dispatched with a warrant signed by New York Mayor Hall (who was himself on trial at the time, charged with fraud) to the *Weekly* office, where they wantonly destroyed furniture while searching for "evidence." All copies of the Beecher issue were confiscated, type scattered and the company books removed. Victoria and Tennie were confined in the Ludlow Street Jail with no trial date set.

An open letter to the *New York Herald* written by Victoria caused many to feel that the government was going too far. It read, in part:

> Sick in body, sick in mind, sick at heart, I write these lines to ask if, because I am a woman, I am to have no justice, no fair play, no chance through the press to reach public opinion. How can anybody know for what I am accused, arrested, imprisoned, unless the public are allowed to see the alleged libel? If the paper is suppressed and I charged with crime, in what way can I substantiate the truth, when the judge before whom I only appear as a witness, constitutes himself as plaintiff, prosecuting attorney, judge, jury and witness? When has it ever been known in this land of so-called religious freedom and civil liberty, that pulpit, press and people tremble before a cowardly opinion?

It was evident that for a time at least, Beecher was—like Caesar's wife—above suspicion. Victoria clearly was not. Still there were some who expressed uneasiness at the workings of the law as applied to her.

Election day came and no votes were cast for Victoria. Yet comfort · came from an unexpected source. Aside from Catherine and Harriet, Beecher had no support from his family. His brother Thomas, also a minister, wrote to another sister, Isabella—who was a great admirer of Victoria's; she addressed her as "Madame Queen"—"I respect Mrs. Woodhull, while I abhor her philosophy. She only carries out Henry's philosophies against which I recorded my protest twenty years ago. . . . Of the two, Woodhull is my hero, and Henry my coward."

The letter ultimately found its way into the newspapers. It was not disowned by the writer. The ranks of the respectable began to waver. *The Hartford Times* states that the Beecher article would never have brought an indictment if it had appeared in the *New York Times*. Suddenly journalists began to take a personal view of civil rights and turned an accusatory eye at Anthony Comstock. The *New York Sunday Mercury* agreed with Victoria when she called Comstock an "illiterate puppy."

A *Mercury* editorial stated: "It does not seem right that the whole machinery of the Federal Government, with its courts and marshals, should be placed at the back of a man who has, somehow or other, chosen it for his private business to deprive this woman of her liberty." The authorities yielded reluctantly—but not for long. Victoria and Tennie were released and immediately rearrested. Three different counts and three different courts were listed. *The Brooklyn Eagle*, published practically in Beecher's backyard and never a friend of Victoria's, now rose to her defense. "We can discover no intention on the part of authorities to try these women at all," it flatly stated. "The seeming disposition to indefinitely incarcerate them is discernible."

December of 1872 came to a close. Victoria and Tennie spent the holidays in the Ludlow Street Jail, but were finally let out on bail early in January. Anthony Comstock marked the new year with the resolution "to do something every day for Jesus." A great opportunity afforded itself on January 9 when he read in the paper that Victoria planned to tell the whole story in a lecture titled, "The Naked Truth," that very evening.

Learning that a stray copy of *Woodhull & Claflin's Weekly* had been sent through the mail, he rushed to the authorities with this new evidence of "obscene literature." Federal authorities were predictably cooperative and an indictment was issued against Victoria, Tennessee and Colonel Blood. Blood was arrested near the brokerage office but managed to warn the others. Tennessee hid under a washtub while Victoria escaped to Jersey City.

New Yorkers attending the lecture braved the winter weather only to be informed by uniformed policemen standing guard at Steinway Hall that Victoria was being sought for arrest and would not be speaking that evening. A few turned away but many more went in anyway. As they sat speculating, a little old lady dressed as a Quaker slipped past fifty policemen and walked up onto the stage. Flinging aside her cloak and coal-scuttle bonnet, she revealed herself to be Victoria Woodhull.

The audience cheered wildly, the police stood by while Victoria spoke, magnificently. It was one of the great moments of her life and she played it to the hilt. One and a half hours later, she bowed to the three United States marshals waiting in the wings. Extending her wrists submissively, she allowed herself to be handcuffed and led away. This time her cellmate at the Ludlow Street Jail was Colonel Blood.

Tennessee later emerged from her washtub and joined them. There was a hearing. This time bail was set and the three were released. Eleven days later the police were back with new warrants. They were taken to the Tombs, one of history's penal horrors.

In court the following day, it was pointed out that the three defendants were now under $60,000 bail for a simple misdemeanor. At the same time Boss Tweed, accused of looting the city's treasury of millions, had been asked for only $51,000 in bail. Though the commissioner was unimpressed with this argument, newspapers rallied to their defense. The charge of issuing an obscene publication was a farce. The story was not obscene. It might have been libelous—if Beecher could have disproved it but he couldn't; Tilton possessed a signed confession from him.

Edward H.G. Clark, editor of the *Troy, New York Whig,* took Beecher's guilt for granted in an editorial stating: "Through these two women, American law has been outraged, the rights of the press assailed, freedom of speech endangered and the functions of the republican government usurped, to cloak the reputation of one or two prominent individuals." Of Victoria, he added, "She ought to be hanged, and then have a monument erected to her memory at the foot of the gallows."

Victoria continued lectures and publication of the *Weekly* despite continuing arrests and arraignments. It was an exhausting process that finally took its toll. She collapsed with a ruptured lung and remained in a coma for several days. She recovered only to be arrested again. Out on bail once more, Victoria encountered family problems and inevitable tragedy. The strange love-hate emotions felt by Utica Claflin for her older sister, Victoria, added to her drinking problems, creating continual havoc. A frequent activity of Utica's was disrupting Victoria's lectures by heckling. Many times the younger woman had to be forcibly removed from the auditorium.

Utica's drinking and emotional scenes continued until another sister, Margaret Ann—who had been struck by a chair during one of the spectacles—had Utica arrested for disorderly conduct. Hauled away screaming, Utica insisted that it was all Victoria's fault. Her mother Roxanna was in vociferous agreement. Once released, Utica frequented the neighborhood saloons where she angrily denounced Victoria for attaining the fame that she believed rightfully belonged to her. She complained bitterly that she had no home and no one to buy her whiskey. Collapsing suddenly, she was carried back to the Claflin residence where she lay in state surrounded by sobbing relatives.

Victoria left the emotion-ridden house one night to catch up on her work at the newspaper. While riding the Broadway omnibus, she noted the clock on the Trinity Church steeple. It read eleven-thirty. At that moment, she heard Utica's voice reassuring her, "Vicky, it's all right now." Victoria understood immediately; her troubled, success-starved sister was at peace at last. Returning home, she found that Utica had died exactly at eleven-thirty. Roxanna, Polly and Margaret Ann were hysterical. Utica must have been poisoned, they insisted, their suspicions centering around Victoria. Acting immediately, Victoria and Tennessee demanded an autopsy. The findings revealed that Utica's death had been caused by Bright's disease aggravated by alcoholism.

Once things at home returned to whatever approached normalcy, Victoria reflected on her seemingly endless legal battles. She asked:

> Do you wonder, that I should feel desperately in earnest to reform the evils of our social life when I remember what I have suffered in my own family? Opposed and misunderstood by my parents and sisters, compelled to bear an idiot child by a drunken husband. Oh, my God! and the world thinks me only ambitious of notoriety.

It was, unfortunately, quite true. Yet everything that Victoria did or said resulted in a continual notoriety that by turns excited and then exhausted her. The decisive trial date was finally set for March 5, 1874. Once the jury was chosen—an almost endless process—the judge showed his bias by refusing bail. Victoria, Tennie and Colonel Blood were returned to their now familiar cells in the Tombs. The same judge allowed testimony to deviate from the case so far that Victoria was asked such questions as, "In your opinion, should a woman desert her husband and live with another man, if prompted by such a desire?"

Waving aside her own counsel's protests, she answered frankly, "If her will takes her away from a man, she surely ought to go. I hold that any man or woman, whether married or unmarried, who consorts for anything but love, is a prostitute."

Nothing but a guilty verdict could be returned Judge Sutherland informed the jury in his summing-up speech. The jurymen retired at noon and returned at 11:05 the following morning. The verdict on their one-hundredth ballot was *Not Guilty*. His Honor was furious as those present in the courtroom burst into spontaneous applause. "It is the most outrageous verdict ever recorded," he roared. "It is shameful and infamous and I am ashamed of the jury who rendered such a verdict!"

Much had happened during the long months of bitter litigation. Beecher's *Life of Jesus* went begging. The publishing company was bankrupt and collections were dwindling rapidly at the Plymouth Church. The sainthood of Henry Ward Beecher was forever sullied. Theodore Tilton walked about with a bound volume of what he referred to as *The True Story*. Once the initial embarrassment had worn off, he seemed to relish his martyred husband role. Always eager to prick a sanctimonious balloon, Victoria reminded the reading public that "After all, Tilton was not exactly a vestal virgin himself." No one questioned her sources. This was a solitary glimmer from Victoria's seemingly flickering candle. Beecher had emerged from the holocaust merely a tarnished angel, while Victoria was totally drained both emotionally and economically. It was the darkest moment of her life.

Wearily she addressed the National Association of Spiritualists at their annual convention. Only a few days before, her forthcoming appearance had been denounced by an active member, S. S. Jones, in his magazine, *The Religio-Philosophical Journal*. Jones took a dim view of Victoria's free love doctrine. Colonel Blood investigated the man, found that he knowingly rented rooms for the purpose of prostitution, reported him to the police and subsequently had him arrested during the convention. The triumph was slight compared to Victoria's depression at meeting just one more obvious case of hypocrisy—this time within the ranks of her most ardent supporters. "Can anyone tell me where I am?" she asked the crowd of spiritualists, staring out over the vast sea of suddenly unfriendly faces. Believing now that she belonged nowhere, Victoria recalled sitting down beside a fashionably dressed woman acquaintance on a New York omnibus. "For heaven's sake, Mrs. Woodhull, do not recognize me," she pleaded. ".'It would ruin my business."

Victoria explained to the audience that her omnibus companion had been a madam concerned that customers might see the two of them conversing. Fearing exposure, they might not patronize her popular house of assignation. "I am ostracized by those whom the world calls prostitutes almost as fearfully as I am by those whom I call the *real* prostitutes," she sighed. A man rose to his feet and accused her of prostituting herself sexually for the cause of suffrage. Victoria drew back in surprise, "A man questioning my virtue!" Just why this came as such a shock to her, no one knew, but all leaned forward in anticipation as she continued: "I declare that I never had sexual intercourse with any man of whom I am ashamed to stand side by side before the world with the act. I am not ashamed of any act in my life. At the time it was the best I knew. Nor am I ashamed of any desire that has been gratified, nor any passion alluded to."

Her head back, her eyes flashing, she answered his charge, "When I came out of prison I came out a beggar. I went to bankers, presidents of railroads, gamblers, prostitutes and got money that has sent you the paper you have been reading; and I do not think that you are the worse for handling it. I used whatever influence I had to get the money and that's my own business and none of yours. And if I devoted my body to my work and my soul to God, that is my business and not yours."

And that wasn't all:

Are there any of you who would have come forward and put

your bodies in the gap? If you will not, don't put me before you as needing to confess anything that in your self-sanctified spirits you may conceive to be prostitution. If I want sexual intercourse with one hundred men, I shall have it!

I am charged with seeking notoriety, but who among you would accept any notoriety and pay a tithe of its cost to me? Driven from my former beautiful home, reduced from affluence to want, my business broken up and destroyed, dragged from one jail to another . . . Now, until you are ready to accept my notoriety, with its conditions—to suffer what I have suffered and am yet ready to suffer—do not dare to impugn my motives. As to your approval or disapproval, your applause or your curses, they have not a feather's weight to me, I am set apart for a high and sacred duty, and I shall perform it without fear or favor.

"Unfit to listen to," was the editorial opinion of the *Chicago Tribune;* but the American Association of Spiritualists once again re-elected Victoria as their president. Unfortunately Victoria's brief happiness in Chicago could not buy money. The brokerage house was closed, soon the *Weekly* ceased publication. It seemed that the wages of Beecher's sins spelled ruin for Victoria as well.

Too exhausted to speak at a meeting of the Philadelphia Spiritualists, Victoria sent her mother and older sister, Margaret Ann, to fulfill the engagement. It was an unfortunate choice. When a speaker criticized Victoria for involving the Spiritualistic movement in her free love cause, a Miss Dunbar rose in her defense and pointed out that Victoria spoke her own sentiments and was not representing any other cause or individual.

Unaccountably enraged, Roxanna leaped to her feet. "Tisn't so! You lie!" she shouted. "My daughters are not responsible for what they say or do. They're psychologized by that devil of a Blood! But they're my daughters and I love them and I'll defend them. But you're a liar!" Not to be outdone, Margaret Ann rushed into the fray, abusing Victoria, Tennessee and Colonel Blood while defending her mother. Roxanna waved her furled umbrella angrily at the audience as she and Margaret Ann were ejected from the hall. *The Philadelphia Record* reported that "the assemblage broke up in the greatest confusion."

Everything now seemed the greatest confusion to Victoria as well. The combined efforts of family and foes were too much for her fragile constitution. Her rare lectures began to focus entirely on menstruation—a topic almost as daring as free love in those Victorian times. It seems likely that Victoria's obsessive concern for the subject coupled with her own now chronic exhaustion indicated a serious physical problem that she could not afford to have corrected. For years Victoria had enjoyed pointing to Colonel Blood as he sat near her on the lecture platform and informing the audience, "There is my lover, but when I cease to love him, I will leave him, though I trust that will never be." But that day had come. At thirty-nine Victoria was again divorced and alone, the sole support of her family.

Then, to the fury of the Beechers and their blind followers, an unexpected event enabled Victoria to rise again. Once more Commodore Vanderbilt catapulted her from oblivion to ascendency. This time the spirit involved was his own. Vanderbilt had died suddenly on the morning of January 4, 1877, leaving an estate of over $100,000,000. William, his favorite son, was to receive $95,000,000. The other son, Cornelius, and his eight daughters were to divide $5,000,000 between them. However the Commodore had also left a modest sum to Victoria and Tennessee to be used for the advancement of spiritualism.

Cornelius and the other outraged minority heirs were determined to contest their father's entire will on the grounds that the old man was mentally incompetent at the time the will was written. Victoria and Tennie C. Claflin, his former spiritual advisors, were obviously promising witnesses for their case. William Vanderbilt was not going to take any chances; Cornelius was quickly allotted an additional $1,000,000 and the Vanderbilt daughters also silenced with settlements. At the same time Victoria and Tennie, who had been totally destitute the month before, departed suddenly for England—each had a ravishing new wardrobe. Six first-class staterooms were booked to accommodate the entourage which included Buck, Roxanna, Zulu Maude and Byron. It would surely seem that the ghost of the Commodore had come back to aid Victoria at the very moment when Demosthenes seems to have deserted her.

Victoria's internal health problems corrected abroad, she was soon back on the lecture platform looking fit and well. This time her subject, "The Human Body," was an impassioned plea to the mothers of London to tell their children the facts of life. Seated in the audience was John Biddulph Martin, a handsome, aristocratic banker, three years younger than herself who fell in love with Victoria at first sight.

"I left the hall that night with the determination that if Mrs. Woodhull would have me, I would certainly make her my wife," he recalled later. The response of Martin's socialite mother was also spirited. "Over my dead body!" she warned. And that's exactly what happened. Victoria and John were married six years later, shortly after the death of his mother. On Halloween, at the age of forty-five, Victoria Claflin Woodhull became the lawful mistress of a stately mansion at 17 Hyde Park Gate. The home was quickly redecorated to suit the fancy of the bride. Demosthenes was not forgotten. There were many marble busts to remind Victoria of the spirit guide who it seems had fortuitously returned to lead her to John Martin.

To the righteous indignation of the moralists back home, the notorious Tennie C. also married happily and well. Her husband was Sir Francis Cook, a wealthy baronet. One wonders what her many male admirers in America thought as they read newspaper accounts of the "blond spirituelle Lady Cook." Tennie was as great a favorite abroad as she had always been—but in a different way. The passing of Lady Cook at seventy-five was greatly mourned by English society which had grown fond of her insouciant ways.

While the staid, conservative Martin may have privately speculated as to what Victoria's behavior might have been before he married her, he remained a gallant knight defending her vigorously in numerous blackmail attempts. He also smiled his approval through spiritualist meetings and three more unsuccessful presidential campaigns. When he died after eighteen years of marriage, Victoria was left with a large estate in Worcestershire and just under two hundred thousand pounds. She had come a long way from Homer, Ohio.

Determined to live life fully to the very end, Victoria tore about the countryside in a white sportscar urging her frightened chauffeur ever faster. At night she sat up in a rocking chair, unwilling to meet death asleep in her bed. She lived to be eighty-nine, aiding the suffrage cause which had somehow grown respectable along with herself. She was responsible for the founding of a woman's college and a progressive village school but these innovations were as nothing compared to the liberal movement which she had almost singlehandedly set into motion.

The inevitable came June 20, 1927, just three months short of her ninetieth birthday. Victoria's obituary was discreet, merely an oblique reference to her influence in the pioneer suffrage movement.

The handful of survivors who recalled her turbulent, troublesome past might have agreed instead with that other editor who had recommended fifty years before that "she be hanged and then have a monument erected to her memory at the foot of the gallows."

2

AMELIA EARHART

Mistress of the Calculated Risk

> Courage is the price that Life exacts for granting peace.
> The Soul that knows it not, knows no release
> From little things;
> Knows not the livid loneliness of fear.
> Nor mountain heights where bitter joy can hear
> The sound of wings.

The poet was Amelia Earhart who first heard the sound of wings as a Red Cross nurse during World War I. From the vantage point of a hospital she observed firsthand what plane crashes did to aviators, but remained determined to fly herself. During life this resolve would make her the most famous woman on earth. Death rendered her an instant folk hero. As a legend who refused to die, she has attained a lasting place in American mythology.

At a time when few people—male or female—had the audacity to buckle themselves into planes as passengers, Earhart was establishing international altitude and distance records. Yet possibly more significant than airborne daring was her courageous stand on sexual and social issues as they related to women of her time. Today, nearly fifty years later, the questions she raised so fearlessly continue to challenge our emotions and our intellects.

From the first, Amelia disdained the traditional feminine role and sought more challenging alternatives. The task was not an easy one. As a child searching for female models among the pages of children's literature, she found none.

"Girls are not expected to join in the fun," she concluded in disgust.

Years later she recalled her frustration at a meeting of librarians. "There are no heroines following the shining paths of romantic adventure, as do the heroes of boys' books. For instance, who ever heard of a girl—a pleasant one—shipping on an oil tanker, say, finding the crew about to mutiny and saving the captain's life (while quelling the mutiny) with a well-aimed pistol shot at the leader of the gang! No, goings on of this sort are left to the masculine characters, to be lived over joyously by the boy readers."

"Of course girls have been reading the so-called 'boys books' ever since there have been such. But consider what it means to do so. Instead of closing the covers with shining eyes and the happy thought, 'That might happen to me someday!' the girl, turning the final page, can only sigh regretfully, 'Oh, dear, that can never happen to me—because I'm not a boy!' "

Abandoning the attempt to find girls or women with

whom to identify among the pages of fact or fiction, Earhart determined very young to make her own history. That she succeeded beyond even her own wildest imaginings was borne out in a presidential address by Herbert Hoover in 1932. The formal affair at Constitution Hall commemorated Amelia's triumph as the first woman to solo across the Atlantic. There would be many other achievements for her but on that occasion Hoover stated that Amelia's flights and courageous manner had combined to place her in the highest tradition of American pioneers.

"Her success," the president said, "has not been won by the selfish pursuits of a purely personal ambition, but as part of a career generously animated by a wish to help others to share in the rich opportunities of life, and by a wish also to enlarge those opportunities by expanding the powers of women as well as men to their ever-widening limits." Such achievements he believed had demonstrated "new possibilities of the human spirit and the human will in overcoming barriers of space and the restrictions of Nature upon the radius of human activity."

President Hoover's reference to the pioneer tradition must have triggered many memories within her. A product of pioneer stock on both sides, Amelia was a curious blend of prestige and plodding, success and sorrow, pride and passion. On her mother's side there were the Otises with their Victorian zeal for material success and social position. Alfred Otis, descending upon the Kansas frontier with his gently reared Philadelphia bride and massive law library, was one of a select few instrumental in establishing the town of Atchison. (His astute sense of timing became apparent when the Santa Fe Railroad designated Atchison as the terminus of its line to the Pacific Coast.) Among Otis' cronies were the editor of the town paper, senators, a state governor and a chancellor of the University of Kansas. His daughter, Amy, was the undisputed belle of the rural community—a good catch by any standards.

Amy's forebears included a young German who, refusing to be docilely conscripted into the king's army as his older brothers had been (all four of whom were subsequently killed in action), defied his militant father and ran away to

sea. Despite his arrival as a penniless young man he ultimately amassed a fortune in the United States. Another spirited antecedent was James Otis who is credited with a
verbal protest against the British Writs of Assistance, referred to by John Adams as the opening gun of the Revolution.
No less a free spirit in her own right, Amy Otis was the first
woman to climb Pike's Peak.

At the opposite end of the spectrum socially and financially was Amelia's grandfather, Reverend David Earhart, a
frontier minister equipped to teach Greek and Hebrew but
totally at a loss to support a wife and twelve children. The
youngest of his progeny was Edwin, an amiable dreamer.
However, Edwin Earhart had his own heritage of independence. In his background was an ancestor who had also
defied parental authority by fleeing Germany. This young
rebel's motivation was the right to marry the woman of his
choice. Equally autonomous, young Edwin had totally disregarded his father's hopes that he enter the ministry, choosing instead to work his way through law school by tutoring
students with more money than brains.

To their ultimate misfortune Amy Otis and Edwin Earhart
literally fell in love at first sight. Alfred Otis tried mightily to
keep the couple apart, insisting that any gentleman who
married his daughter "must be able to show an income of at
least fifty dollars a month with the prospect of increasing
that considerably as time goes on." This demand proved a
sizable barrier in those pre-inflation times, but Amy and
Edwin were not to be dissuaded.

Edwin worked five years before he could meet Alfred Otis'
exacting standards. Despite much parental pressure and the
blandishments of numerous suitors, Amy waited patiently.
But unfortunately once they married the romantic glow
faded. One of their daughters, Muriel Earhart Morrissey,
years later delicately referred to a "period of adjustment" for
the couple. "The transition from pampered debutante to
poor man's wife was made with some tears and some unhappy hours," she admitted.

Amelia's reaction to her parents' mismatch was marked by
a lifelong contempt for security. She was consistently outspoken in her statement that the potential of many able

women was destroyed by their attempts to get through life in the safest, most comfortable way—through a man. Further, as Amelia saw it, this "stunted" wife was yoked to a man whose creativity was drained away by her demands. Thus the woman who perceived her identity solely as a wife had no other standard of achievement but the tokens of material success earned by this man. Amelia who has been described a "mistress of the calculated risk" determined very early not to fall into the same trap.

She and her younger sister, Muriel, watched as their father sacrificed his dreams of a political career for a safe income as a railroad claims adjuster. When a measure of success came to Edwin, admiring new companions and ready cash proved more than he could handle. The son of a poor clergyman who had once boasted "there was not a drunkard among the whole of our kin," soon developed a penchant for alcohol that could not be controlled. The brief period of affluence ended with his demotion to railroad clerk.

Despite their many personal problems, Amy and Edwin were open-hearted, open-minded parents who placed few restrictions on their daughters. Amy bought the girls bloomers so that they could play any game that boys could play. Edwin gave them footballs for Christmas and at nine Amelia received a rifle with which she successfully controlled the rat population in the Earhart barn.

Life was not so freewheeling during the long periods spent with their maternal grandmother—exiles necessitated by Edwin's financial vicissitudes. Later Amelia was to speak of those days with some resentment. "I know that I worried my grandmother considerably by running home from school and jumping over the fence which surrounded her home. Probably if I'd been a boy, such a shortcut would have been entirely natural. I am not suggesting that girls jump out of their cribs and begin training, but only that the pleasure from exercise might be enhanced if they knew how to do correctly all the things they can do without injuring themselves or giving a shock to their elders. Of course, I admit that some_ elders have to be shocked for everybody's good now and then."

In school Amelia was an apt pupil but unimpressed by praise. A teacher once remarked of her, "The joy of achievement was uppermost in Amelia's mind. The prizes at school as the plaudits and awards of the world were secondary to her personal satisfaction in a job well done." This trait was apparent throughout life. Amelia's many flying trophies and medals were never displayed in her Rye, New York home.

Also, although she was egalitarian in her concern for others, social triumphs or travails seemed of little importance. Her refusal to play the coquette, to assume a helpless stance to entice the boys made for a few lonely evenings. "I don't think that boys cared particularly for me," she recalled later, "but I can't remember being very sad about the situation. Probably I didn't get so much exercise at dancing as I would have liked, because of having only one or two faithful partners." Much as she loved her kindly, befuddled father, he had provided a negative model of manhood. The effect upon his oldest daughter was the emergence of a strong personality, an individualist who could function happily with or without a man.

Dependent at that point upon the bounty of relatives for much of her sustenance, Amelia determined to get the best high school education possible—reasoning that it might well be the end of her formal training. Discovering that the chemistry laboratory of her neighborhood school was nothing more than "a kitchen sink," the teenager set about interviewing several high school principals in Chicago where the family was then living. Most of the facilites were found wanting, but at last she selected Hyde Park High School. Though miles from home, adequate chemistry and physics courses were offered there.

Unfortunately even a girl with the foresight of Amelia Earhart could not anticipate everything. Frustrated as many bright students have been and still are by educational bureaucracy, she fumed as her time was wasted by a totally incompetent teacher. The elderly woman's deafness made it impossible for her to do more than go through the motions of teaching English; no effort was made to follow a study plan or to discuss the literature of the past or present. Most of the class took advantage of the time to joke and gossip. Amelia's attempt to rectify the situation by circulating a petition among the group proved a failure. Few of the teenagers were farsighted enough to exchange an amusement period for disciplined study and the administration was unwilling to remove a teacher "only a few years from retirement." Rather than waste more time in the riotious classroom, Amelia demanded and received permission to spend English period in the school library where she read four times the number of required books for the course. When the Class of '16 marched to the platform at graduation, Amelia refused to take part in the ceremony. She had no further use for Hyde Park High School. It is no surprise that the caption under her yearbook picture read, "The girl in brown who walks alone."

One wonders what went on in Amelia's mind years later when Mayor Cermak of Chicago pressed the belated high school diploma on her at a ceremony honoring one of her many triumphs. "I give you this diploma, as of 1916, Miss Earhart, not that you need this small honor you earned sixteen years ago, but that we want you to have it so the world will know you belong to us," he explained. Amelia gave him a brief smile. The year was 1932, speech then was less free than today, and Amelia—brave and innovative as she was—was still the product of a late Victorian society. Today her reply might well have been "bullshit."

Fortunately when Earhart started college in the fall of 1916, attending Ogontz School in Rydal, Pennsylvania, she finally found the intellectual stimulation that she craved. Miss Abby Sutherland, headmistress of Ogontz, described her as a girl always pushing into unknown seas in her reading. "The look in her straightforward, eager eyes was most fascinating in those days," Miss Sutherland said. "Her most characteristic charm was her poise, her reserve, her curiosity."

During her college days Amelia busied herself by filling a scrapbook with stories and pictures of women throughout the world who were taking over jobs thought to be the realm of men. These newspaper accounts were livened by her own penciled comments. After a quote from Helen H. Gardner, the first woman to become United States Civil Service Commissioner, describing the simultaneous conducting of home and job as difficult but not impossible, Amelia wrote in: "Good girl, Helen!" Unimpressed by the legislation then being proposed to permit women to own property the remarkably self-possessed Earhart commented: "This method is not sound. Women will gain economic justice by proving themselves in all lines of endeavor, not having laws passed for them."

On the other hand, she was impatient with the restrictions of college sororities. After being odd girl out at Hyde Park, it had been pleasant to be sought after and pledged to one of the three secret sororities on campus. "Sisterhood" was important to her, she enjoyed the camaraderie with other women and the exchange of ideas; but the thought that some were left out of the fun bothered her. When others in her group refused to take in more members, she approached the headmistress and suggested that the faculty approve a fourth sorority so that more women could take part. "Every girl should have the fun of belonging to a sorority if she wants to," she insisted. Once again her one woman crusade was a failure. College women were no more willing to forfeit their exclusivity than high school students their amusement and the college establishment was equally wary of challenge.

Amelia did not graduate from Ogontz. With World War I peaking, it was inevitable that she would be drawn to more immediate issues. While visiting Muriel at St. Margaret's College in Toronto in the spring of 1917 Amelia had ample opportunity to view the wounded pouring back from the trenches. The sight of three young British soldiers on crutches with but three legs between them was too much for her. "There for the first time," she later wrote, "I realized what the World War meant. Instead of new uniforms and brass bands, I saw the results of four years' desperate struggle; men without arms and legs, men who were paralyzed and men who were blind." Anxious to do something to relieve some of the suffering she was witnessing daily, Amelia enrolled in a Voluntary Aid Detachment and was sent to a military hospital. She proved a hardworking, highly efficient nurse, compassionate of pain but cool in time of need. She also possessed a keen sense of humor that made her a general favorite at the hospital. Listening to pilots speak longingly of their airborne adventures, she longed to fly herself. And with Amelia thought and action were never far separated.

However when the war ended she entered Columbia University as a premedical student. Her abilities in the lab greatly impressed a biology professor, James MacGregor, who later expressed the opinion that had Amelia not become caught up in the adventure of flying, she would have conquered equally challenging frontiers in the laboratory. His pupil was doubtful about medicine as a career. She would recall, "It took me only a few months to discover that I probably should not make the ideal physician. Though I liked learning all about medicine, particularly the experimental side, visions of its practical application floored me. For instance, I thought among other possibilities of sitting at the bedside of a hypochondriac and handing out innocuous sugar pellets to a patient with an imaginary illness. 'If you'll take these pills,' I heard myself saying in a professional tone, 'the pain in your knee will be much less, if not entirely eliminated.' This picture made me feel inadequate and insecure."

Addressing herself to a different problem, she left Columbia after one year and followed her parents to California where Edwin Earhart's will-o-wisp fortunes had taken them. By now her parents' union was near dissolution. They hoped that Amelia's presence might perform a domestic miracle. "Finish your education in California," her parents urged.

Instead their daughter signed up for flying lessons after securing a job with the Los Angeles telephone company to finance the $1,000 fee. "From then on," she recalled later, "the family scarcely saw me for I worked all week and spent what I had of Saturday and Sunday at the airport a few miles from town." (A "few miles" to Amelia involved an hour's ride by streetcar and then a walk of several miles along Wilshire Boulevard, which was at that time merely a barren expanse of sagebrush and rabbit holes.) The inconvenience mattered very little. Amelia took to every aspect of flying, quickly adopting breeches and a leather coat. Her hair was cropped to accommodate the wind. "Some day we're going to have planes with covered cockpits so a pilot won't have to be blown to pieces," she told her sister. In the meantime, Amelia happily accepted flying as it was, in spite of the wobbly Army surplus training planes then in use.

Some of her enthusiasm was engendered by her instructor, Neta Snook. "Snooky," Amelia reported to her family, "dresses and talks like a man and can do everything around a plane that a man can do. I'm lucky that she'll teach me, not only because she will give me lessons on credit, but because she is a top-notch flier." Even Snooky couldn't match Amelia's optimism for the future of aviation. "I'm sure we'll have planes large enough to carry ten or a dozen passengers and they'll go on regular schedules like trains," the happy pupil prophesied.

The pioneer blood of the Earhart clan must have quickened at Amelia's vision and courage. Despite their natural fears for her, Amy and Muriel came to her financial assistance. On July 24, 1922—Amelia's twenty-fifth birthday—she took possession of a small biplane that they had helped her purchase at much sacrifice to themselves. Three months later she set a women's altitude record by flying at 14,000 feet.

During this period, Amelia became involved with Samuel Chapman, a young engineer who wanted her to marry him. Muriel, in her biography, *Courage in the Price*, recalls that Sam mistakenly imagined that Amelia's reluctance stemmed from his irregular hours as an engineer. "I'll be whatever you want me to be. I'll get other work tomorrow if you say so," he pleaded. Amelia's response was annoyance. "I don't want to tell Sam what he should do. He ought to *know* what makes him happiest, and then do it, no matter what other people say. I know what I want to do, and I expect to do it, married or single!"

Muriel, writing from the vantage point of motherhood and many years of marriage, acknowledged her sister's independence in refusing Sam. "I believe her reluctance to continue the engagement stemmed from Sam's outspoken disapproval of working wives. His stern Yankee upbringing had impressed upon him the importance of the man's role as breadwinner and protector of his wife; since he was able to support a wife and family, he expected to do it."

Not caring for a life of domesticity and not able to find a career at the time in aviation, Amelia became a social worker. She was rehearsing a settlement house play in Boston when a telephone call came from a stranger who would change the course of her life. Imagining that it was just another bootlegger urging her to fly liquor in from Canada, Amelia answered brusquely.

"Would you like to do something important for the cause of aviation?" a man's voice inquired.

"Such as what?"

"Flying across the Atlantic."

"Yes," she answered without hesitation. "How could I refuse such a shining adventure?"

It was 1928, only a few months after Lindbergh's historic Atlantic crossing. A wealthy American woman living in England wanted another flight made as a symbol of good will between the two countries. She had purchased a plane, to be called the *Friendship*, and would finance the venture. The pilot was to receive $20,000, the mechanic $5000. The woman passenger they were seeking would be flight "captain," yet her only compensation would be the privilege of making the trip. The title was nebulous, the danger was not. Added to the risk implicit in the pioneer attempt was an alcoholic pilot—but this Amelia would discover later.

In the meantime she had to be screened by Capt. Hilton Railey (who had called her) and his friend, publisher G.P. Putnam who had been entrusted with the task of finding the female captain. Her meeting with them in New York proved to be a mental and emotional obstacle course almost as great as flying the Atlantic. "I think we talked for an hour, more about my education and work and hobbies than about flying," she related later. "I had the feeling that if they liked me too much they wouldn't want me to make such a hazardous flight but if they didn't like me enough they would let me make it. I realized that they were making me talk to see whether I dropped my g's or used 'ain't,' which I'm sure would have disqualified me as effectively as failing to produce my pilot's license. Mediocrity seemed to be my cue, so that's what they got."

Amelia did not have to wait long for their decision. It was decided unanimously that she would make the flight. The pilot, Wilmer (Bill) Stultz, and navigator, Louis (Slim) Gordon had already been selected. Now plans for the flight moved swiftly and secretly, for it had been decided that no one was to know of the venture until the three were underway. Amelia was careful to leave her affairs in order. Letters were entrusted to a friend for delivery only in the event that she "popped off." They remained unopened until her death many years and many flights later.

To her mother, Amelia wrote: "Our family tends to be too secure. My life has really been very happy and I don't mind contemplating its end in the midst of it."

To her father: "Hooray for the last grand adventure. I wish I had won but it was worthwhile anyway. You know that. I have no faith that we'll meet anywhere again, but I do wish we might."

On June 4, 1928, they departed on the first lap of the venture. A few hours later they landed in Trepassey Bay, Newfoundland to await favorable weather conditions. It proved a long and arduous ordeal. As the days passed and fog continued to hover about them, Amelia became grimly aware that Bill was far more than a social drinker. Each day he consumed more than a fifth of brandy. It must have seemed ironic to realize that here was another man—for this crucial period the most important individual in her life—with a drinking problem.

At home, the Earhart family was besieged by eager reporters wanting to know everything about Amelia. Mrs. Earhart was almost as horrified by the sudden notoriety as she was by the knowledge of her daughter's undertaking—which she learned now for the first time. "In my day, *nice* people had their names in the paper only when they were born, married and died," she sniffed.

Finally on June 17, twelve days after landing at Trepassey, the *Friendship* was at last able to take off. As she watched the ground fade from view Amelia jettisoned Bill's whiskey which she had discovered hidden from view between the ribs of the fuselage and a tool kit. The flight took twenty hours, forty minutes in its entirety. Bill was kept too busy to miss his bottle.

For Amelia, there was time to marvel at the beauty of the stratosphere. In her log book, she jotted: "I do believe we are getting out of the fog, marvelous shapes in white stand out, some trailing shimmering veils. The clouds look like icebergs in the distance. It seemed almost impossible that one couldn't bounce forever on the packed fog we are leaving. The highest peaks of the fog mountains are tinted pink with the setting sun. The hollows are gray and shadowy."

But after a time the radio gave out and the *Friendship* was totally alone and beginning to run low on fuel. At one point Amelia attempted to attract the attention of the *S.S. America* which was sailing hundreds of feet below them. Hoping that the ship could give some indication of their location, she wrote a quick note, weighted with two oranges and wrapped in a handkerchief, and dropped it from the plane. Amelia missed her target and the fuel was too low to try for a second bombing. There was less than an hour's supply of gas as they continued onward in the same direction.

Fog and rain added to the dilemma, but at last a break in the mist revealed land. The arrival of the *Friendship* at Burryport, Wales hardly raised an eyebrow among the staid fisherfolk who were oblivious to the clamor that had accompanied the flight in other parts of the world. The *Friendship* crew bobbed about in the bay in their pontooned craft until a few dignitaries finally rowed out to inquire what they wanted. Those few hours were the last quiet moments that they would spend for some time; from then on all of Britain went wild with excitement. Amelia who had been only a passenger was embarrassed by the tumultuous cheers and blazing headlines. Again and again she referred to herself as a back seat driver or worse, a sack of potatoes, but few would listen. She felt herself to be sailing—or flying—under false colors but determined to ultimately justify herself by flying the Atlantic solo.

In the meantime she was kept busy outfitting herself from the bottom up. (Amelia's entire luggage for the crossing had consisted of two scarfs, a toothbrush and comb. One of the scarfs had been ripped off by a "fan.")

"Should you like to meet the Prince of Wales?" was the first question asked Amelia. (He was then considered the world's most eligible bachelor.)

"That depends upon his Highness' wishes," an American official quickly answered for her. Amelia said not a word on the subject herself, considering his reply correct and satisfactory. The next day an English daily published her supposed reply:

"Wal, I sure am glad to be here, and gosh, I sure do hope I'll meet the Prince of Wales."

The two did not meet on that trip. Amused, Amelia could readily understand why.

Back home Amelia discovered immediately that she, as the first woman to cross the Atlantic by air, had caught the imagination of the entire nation. Hundreds of offers for personal appearances, speaking tours, radio programs, motion pictures, articles, books, endorsements, and business affiliations came pouring in. One of the very first was the invitation from *McCall's Magazine* to serve as aviation editor. Amelia enthusiastically accepted.

Then came another request that stood out among many and brought her unwanted notoriety. Though Amelia did not smoke herself, she agreed to endorse a brand of cigarettes, with the understanding that her fee would be given to Commander Byrd for his second Antarctic expedition. Amelia's smiling face and competent hands—holding a cigarette—caused a major furor. Cigarette smoking women were considered very daring in 1929 and for that reason conventional women's magazines refused both liquor and tobacco advertising. Concerned about the effect that Amelia's seeming boldness might have upon its editorial image, *McCall's* canceled her contract.

By the time the conservative *McCall's* staff was ready to "reconsider" the decision, *Cosmopolitan* had already snapped at the opportunity to hire a celebrity writer. Amelia was signed to do a minimum of eight articles a year and given an office for her use. The office came in handy for letter answering as well as article writing. Soon Amelia was deluged with correspondence. "I have quarreled with my boy friend and have decided to take up aviation. Please tell me how," one asked. Another complained, "I want to fly but my mother won't let me. She says I should wait until I am older."

"Why not *now*?" Amelia challenged the mother of the latter writer; but admonished the former: "No one should take up flying with what appears to be suicidal thoughts!"

Other letter writers were less friendly: "Since you smoke, I suppose you drink also." (She didn't.) "Cigarette smoking is to be expected from any woman who cuts her hair like a man's and who wears trousers in public."

Undaunted, Amelia turned out a series of articles with such titles as: "Why are Women Afraid to Fly?" "Try Flying Yourself," "Is it Safe for You to Fly?" In one of the same issues was an article by another writer titled, "I Wish I Was a Man." It seems unlikely that Amelia ever entertained such thoughts. She was much too busy being herself.

Between deadlines she was busy flying about the country lecturing. "That initial flight of mine across the continent proved to be a pleasant interlude," Amelia wrote of her 1929 flight in her biography, *The Fun of It.* "I later found that it marked the first solo trip a woman had made from the Atlantic to the Pacific and back again. But at the time it was to me primarily a vacation—a minor adventure in vagabonding by air and a relaxation from writer's cramp."

Later that year Amelia set a new speed record for women over a one mile distance and a few months later established the international speed record over a 100-kilometer course.

Turning now from magazine writing and competitive flying to the development of commercial air lines, she was employed by Transcontinental Air Transport, the corporate parent of the forerunner of TWA, to do public relations. Amelia's job was to combat the popular family excuse for not traveling by air, *Father won't fly if Mother says he can't.* Suddenly the ten-passenger planes that had seemed impossible just eight years before were an actuality. Amelia was to encourage people to use them. When not lecturing about the joy of flying to large groups, she was busy onboard roving up and down the cramped aisles reassuring the few intrepid souls willing to chance air travel.

Amelia's own fears were of another sort. George Putnam,

the publisher who had found the girl to fly the Atlantic had also found the woman he wanted to marry. Through the years he managed to become her closest adviser and had proposed to her five times between 1928 and 1930. Alarmed at the prospect, Amelia confided to her sister, "I can think of lots of things worse than never getting married. One of the worse is being married to a man who tied you down." Putnam's sixth proposal occurred in a hangar while Amelia waited for her plane to warm up. She listened gravely, nodded her head in agreement, patted his arm, jumped into her plane and flew away.

On their wedding day, February 7, 1931, Amelia presented Putnam with a declaration of independence. It read:

> There are some things that should be writ before we are married. Things we talked over before—most of them. You must know again my reluctance to marry, my feeling that I shatter thereby chances in work which means so much to me. I feel the move just now as foolish as anything I could do. I know there may be compensations but have no heart to look ahead.
>
> In our life together I shall not hold you to any medieval code of faithfulness to me, nor shall I consider myself bound to you similarly. If we can be honest I think the differences which arise may best be avoided. Please let us not interfere with each other's work or play, nor let the world see private joys or disagreements. In this connection I may have to keep some place where I can go to be by myself now and then, for I cannot guarantee to endure at all times the confinement of even an attractive cage. I must exact a cruel promise, and this is that you will let me go in a year if we find no happiness together. I will try to do my best in every way.

Though the year passed and the marriage continued, Earhart retained her maiden name, and her ambition. She would reach for the stars until the very end.

Amelia's choice was not necessarily a popular one with her friends or family. Mrs. Earhart opposed the marriage because Putnam was twelve years older and a divorced man. (He had divorced his third wife in order to be free to pursue Amelia.) She did not attend the ceremony held in the home of Putnam's mother in Noank, Connecticut. Although Amelia never sought attention or feigned helplessness as a means of attracting men, she had become extremely popular with them. At least two, Sam Chapman and Hilton Railey, were bitterly disappointed by the marriage.

Many who knew Earhart and Putnam well predicted disaster. Wealthy, talented and considered somewhat spoiled, Putnam was an attractive, outgoing man who loved the limelight. Amelia was thirty-two years old and staunchly individualistic, unwilling to subordinate any of her personal goals. Could Putnam content himself with the role of hero's husband, waiting quietly on the sidelines? Most doubted it.

Muriel did not attend the small ceremony, but responded to Amelia's telegraphed announcement with a message of love and good wishes. She admitted later that she was aware that the principals realized fully the possible mishaps awaiting them. "Perhaps it was because both Amelia and GP realized the hazards of their course that they avoided many danger spots by using intelligence and tolerance in their relationships," Muriel wrote. "They both had consuming interests, distinct from each other: Amelia's, writing, lecturing, flying; GP's publishing books about other people's adventures. They had much in common, too. They shared a love of the world of books, good theater, music and art. Both enjoyed people. GP claimed friendship with men and women famous in many fields and Amelia delighted in knowing those who had done the unusual."

For her own part, Amelia frequently referred to marriage as an affair of mutual responsibility. "I cannot see why husbands shouldn't share in the responsibility of the home," she said. "By that I mean something more detailed—and for as long as it takes them to get used to the idea, perhaps more arduous, even uncomfortable to the men—than merely keeping a roof over the collective head and coal in the furnace."

On the subject of marital finances she stated:

> For the woman to pay her own way may add immeasurably to the happiness of those concerned. The individual independence of dollars and cents tends to keep a healthy balance of power in the kingdom of the home. If one's time is worth more at specialized tasks—writing, flying, interior decorating, what have you—it is good sense to put one's hours at

such work rather than cooking, cleaning and mending. Assistants more skilled than myself can be employed to substitute in the housewife role without robbing a marriage of its essence.

It is fortunately no longer a disgrace to be undomestic, and married women should be able to seek, as unrestrictedly as men, any gainful occupation their talents and interests make available. Thus—for me—can joyful luxuries like low-wing monoplanes be had—as adding to the sum total of contentment.

Putnam and Amelia put this policy to practice by sharing a joint bank account to which each contributed a share to the support of the household, medical bills, car maintenance, trips, etc.

Amelia proved equally outspoken on the subject of a career, insisting, "the more one does and sees and feels, the more one is able to do, and the more genuine may be one's appreciation of fundamental things like home, love and understanding companionship." Her own appreciation of home must have been very high for Amelia ventured very far doing, seeing and feeling all that the world had to offer.

On May 20, 1932 she once again crossed the Atlantic, but this time totally alone. Bernt Balchen, an Arctic explorer and pioneer pilot, served as technical adviser, preparing her plane and flight plan. Later he recalled her arrival at the field just prior to take off, wearing jodhpurs and a leather jacket, her close-cropped blond hair tousled. She was quiet and unassuming, listening calmly as he warned her of the weather to anticipate. Afterward she looked at him with a small, lonely smile and asked "Do you think I can make it?"

He grinned back, "You bet," and watched admiringly as she crawled calmly into the cockpit of the big empty airplane, started the engine, ran it up, checked the mags, and nodded her head. The chocks were pulled and she was off.

On May 21st, Amelia landed in Ireland, the first woman to solo the Atlantic.

This time Amelia did meet the Prince of Wales, who prolonged her visit far beyond the usual audience prescribed by protocol. He asked question after question about the flight.

"I envy you your freedom in flying," he sighed as she at last took her leave, adding, "British tradition is hard to circumvent."

Others were not so enthusiastic. One English columnist characterized her as "unwomanly." Unconcerned by the label, Amelia went on to even greater feats. She was the first individual to solo from Honolulu to California and from the United States round trip to Mexico City. When others marveled at the risks she took, Amelia philosophically explained, "A fatal accident to a woman pilot is not a greater disaster than one to a man of equal worth. Feminine flyers have never subscribed to the super-sentimental valuation placed upon their necks. I am sure they feel they can endure their share of misfortune, whatever it be, as quietly as men."

One who shared her views was Ruth Nichols, a close friend and co-founder of The 99's—a sorority of the air, still active today. "After her marriage to George Palmer Putnam, Amelia became a Rye neighbor and as a result it was easy to visit each other on the spur of the moment," Nichols recalls in her biography, *Wings for Life*. "We were united by a common bond of interest. We spoke each other's language—and that was the language of pioneer women of the air."

"I suppose after Amelia's marriage to Putnam I may have felt a few twinges of envy that she was able always to obtain the latest and finest planes while I had to search for backers for every flight I undertook. But I knew also that there was no bitterness in my envy. I liked and admired her and I believe she felt the same way about me."

"That Amelia always seemed to manage to beat me to the starting line in record flights that both of us were planning was merely the fall of the cards. I felt then and I feel now that the achievements of any flyer, man or woman, advance the science of aviation and so are of eventual benefit to all civilizations."

"Both Amelia and I had crack ups and successes. We both won a lot and lost a lot. But we were privileged to have places in the starting lineup of our country's women flyers, and each of us fulfilled her destiny as she saw it."

Accepting the theory of equality in death, both women pilots demanded equality in life. "It has always seemed to

me that boys and girls are educated very differently,"
Earhart pointed out. "Even from early grades, they take different subjects. For instance, boys are usually put into
woodworking classes and girls into sewing or cooking—
willy-nilly. I know many boys who should, I am sure, be
making pies and girls who are better fitted for manual training than domestic science. Too often little attention is paid to
individual talent. Instead, education goes on dividing people
according to their sex and putting them in little feminine or
masculine pidgeonholes."

Hoping to play a significant part in the changing of all this,
Amelia accepted a professorship at Purdue University. She
lived for six months in one of the women's dormitories,
keeping her doors open to anyone who might want to talk
with her. In the dining hall, she sat with a different group at
every meal. Drawing from her own experiences, she discussed the critical need for the stimulation of competition
outside the home. "A girl must nowadays believe completely
in herself as an individual," she said. "She must realize at
the outset that a woman must do the same job better than a
man to get as much credit for it. She must be aware of the
various discriminations, both legal and traditional, against
women in the business world."

There were many sides to Amelia Earhart—adventurer,
woman's advocate. She dutifully admired her young neph-
ew but obviously preferred children for other people. ("If it
just didn't take so long to make a baby. There are so many
exciting things to be done," she once confided to her sister.)
And there was the romantic, poetic woman, who designed
pretty clothes, rhapsodized about lights and star formations
and wrote passionate poetry to her husband:

> To touch your hand or see your face, today
> Is Joy. Your casual presence in a room
> Recalls the stars that watched us as we lay.
> I mark you in the moving crowd
> And see again those stars
> A warm night lent us long ago.
> We loved so then—we loved so now.

There would be one more long flight, she decided. Not

that she ever intended retirement, but perhaps a slowing down. . . . "It would be nice to actually have time to *see* a place," she'd often remarked. All of her travels had been of necessity whirlwind affairs. Sunshine, lots of books, leisure waited at the end of the rainbow as Amelia planned the greatest challenge of her life. It would be aviation's Everest—a flight around the world. There had been other trans-world flights, but no one had attempted the most difficult equatorial route. It was considered impossible by most, but to Amelia the challenge seemed worth the risk.

To the world she announced: "When I have finished this job I mean to give up long-distance 'stunt' flying. I'm getting old. I want to make way for the younger generation before I'm feeble."

To Putnam she urged: "Please don't be concerned. It just seems that I must try this flight. I've weighed it all out carefully. With it behind me, life will be fuller and richer. I can be content. Afterward, it will be fun to grow old." It seems doubtful that it would have. A vicarious armchair existence appears inconsistent with Earhart's life-long search for new and greater personal challenges.

She had once explained to Louise Thaden, then a young neophyte pilot with scarcely one hundred solo air hours, "We women pilots have a rough rocky road ahead of us. Each accomplishment, no matter how small, is important. Although it may be no direct contribution to the science of aeronautics nor to its technical development, it will encourage other women to fly. The more who become pilots, the quicker will we be recognized as an important factor in aviation."

The two became close friends and confidants. Viewing Amelia as the years passed, Thaden reported in her autobiography, *High, Wide and Frightened*, "Like the rest of us, Amelia had ambitions. Unlike most of us she had a definite notion of each progressive step toward the set goal. Never swerving from the beacon ahead, she climbed the stairs, step by step. Discouragement, frustration, hundreds of smaller obstacles, but probably most of all, loneliness could not deter her ascending the high pinnacle of predetermined achievement."

"It may seem incongruous, yet AE's personal ambitions were secondary to an insatiable desire to get women into the air; and once in the air to have the recognition she felt they deserved accorded them." That she believed was the basic reason for Amelia's second Atlantic crossing, her record trials and race competitions, and her Pacific flight. But the round-the-world flight appeared to be different she said—it was undertaken for "fun."

"I've worked hard," Amelia confided, "and I deserve *one* fling during my lifetime." She laughed as her friend Thaden attempted to dissuade her by suggesting that water lilies would be an appropriate floral tribute. Then turning serious, Earhart said, "If I *should* bop off it would be doing the thing I've always wanted to do. Being a fatalist yourself, you know the Man with the little black book has a date marked down for all of us—when our work is finished."

On May 20, 1937, Amelia Earhart set off for her grand adventure. With her was Fred Noonan, who would act as navigator. Once again she entrusted her life to an alcoholic. A former Pan Am pilot, Noonan had been suspended as a bad risk. His association with Earhart was in the nature of a comeback; he had sworn off liquor and gotten married just before leaving on the historic flight.

Amelia and Noonan had traversed thousands of miles of sea, uncharted wastes and heavily fortified restricted areas when they finally touched down in Karachi, then a part of India. "There's a phone call for you," Amelia was told as she walked wearily away from the plane.

"Yes," she sighed, certain that it was yet another interviewer.

"It's from New York, Mr. Putnam on the wire."

Amelia rushed inside and grabbed the phone.

From 8,000 miles away, her husband asked, "How do you feel?"

"Fine, a little tired perhaps."

"How's the ship?"

"Everything seems O.K. There's been a little trouble with the fuel flow meter and analyzer, but I think they'll cure that here."

"How's Fred?"

"Fine . . ."

"Having a good time?"

"Oh, yes," she answered. "It's been very worthwhile. We'll do it again together some time."

"O.K. with me. Anything else?"

"Well, I'll cable tomorrow with an estimate of when we should get into Howland. Good-by . . . See you in Oakland."

Two days later the plane was pronounced ready and they set off across the subcontinent for Calcutta. Sand and rain storms marked the 1,300 mile trip. It was pouring rain as they reached Dum Dum Airport. The monsoons that Amelia had hoped to avoid had already begun. Sheet after sheet of heavy rain made the flight from Calcutta to Rangoon an endurance test for plane and pilot. Flying at 8,000 feet in an effort to escape the storm, Amelia's eyes were constantly on the instruments. Her whole body ached as she attempted to keep the nose of the plane up, the wings level.

At last the weather cleared and she was able to catch a glimpse of the Irrawaddy River and finally the golden peaks of the Shwe Dagon Pagoda below. They landed, intending only to refuel but just as they touched ground another downpour engulfed them making take-off impossible. It was another two days before they were able to leave for Bangkok and once again driving rain followed them all the way.

En route eastward out of Bangkok, Earhart was plagued with engine troubles and malfunctioning navigational instruments. At last arriving at Lae, New Guinea on June 30, Amelia was exhausted from the strain. Flying 22,000 miles in only forty days had taken its toll. Her last written message was a wistful desire "to stay here peacefully for a time and see something of this strange and appealing land." Just before leaving New Guinea to begin the longest leg of the world flight—the 2,556-mile jump to Howland Island,—she wrote, "I shall be glad when we have the hazards of its navigation behind us."

On July 2, Amelia took off for Howland, in the Pacific due west of the Gilbert Islands. Across the International Dateline where they were headed it was one day later but two hours earlier by the sun. By 8 a.m. the next day, twenty hours had elapsed since their departure and Amelia and Noonan were two hours overdue.

The crew of the Coast Guard cutter *Itasca*, who were to guide them to Howland, grew anxious, frantic and finally despairing. They could hear Amelia's voice requesting directions but she apparently could not receive their answer. Again and again they signaled their location and asked for hers but the air waves remained silent.

By noon there was no question that the plane's fuel supply would have run out. It was fervently hoped by all that Earhart had managed to land somewhere. Lacking that "they can stay afloat indefinitely," Putnam optimistically wired from San Francisco. "Their empty tanks will give them buoyancy. Besides they have all the emergency equipment they'll need—everything."

An all-out search began but it netted nothing. Amelia and Noonan had disappeared into the Pacific. Endless speculation through the years regarding the cause of her disappearance merely adds to Amelia's incredible legend. Yet how she died is not nearly so important as why she died.

"Please know I am aware of the hazards," Amelia wrote to her husband just before her last great adventure. "I want to do it because I must do it. Women must try to do things as men have tried. When they fail, their failure must be but a challenge to others."

3

ISADORA DUNCAN

A Force of Nature

Isadora Duncan literally made history every day of her life.

Yesterday and tomorrow meant nothing. What counted was living today to the utmost. For her compromise did not—could not—exist. In its place was a passion for life and a genius for causing trouble.

Her creative dancing, experimental schools, numerous lovers and revolutionary politics made her the most controversial artist of the 20th century and left in her wake a legend of glamor, eccentricity and stark drama.

It is impossible to separate Isadora's personal life from her career. She was from the beginning a dynamic innovator who dared to live and love as she chose. The results, sometimes disastrous, were dutifully chronicled in headlines that blazed across continents. She was called the "female Casanova of America" and the "greatest courtesan of our times" by intimate associates. Another admirer, Lloyd Morris, wrote, "Though her love affairs sprang from passion, she conducted them on principle. Every time she took another lover she made herself believe that this was Love Himself at last. All the others had been mere ambassadors and now the hour of fulfillment was at hand."

Isadora relished the good life, but was anything but materialistic. She tormented her loves but never victimized them. She gave herself completely, without reserve, asking nothing in a monetary sense. Her lovers were as varied as her whims—actors, businessmen, poets, designers, musicians, and wastrels of all kinds. If there was gold digging involved,

she was the gold, not the digger.

"I never leave my lovers; they leave me," she boasted frequently. Yet it is difficult to believe that one man could have been enough for long. She, herself, compared a woman who has had only one lover to a musician who has listened to but one composer. Returning to San Francisco—the city of her birth—on tour, she encountered a love from her·early youth and discovered to her surprise that he was still in love with the simple unsophisticated woman that he had married long ago. Her reaction was pity. How could such a thing be, she wondered, her amazement tingled with contempt.

As she neared the half-century mark Isadora looked back over her chaotic life and decided with some satisfaction that it had been more interesting than any novel and more adventurous than any cinema. When asked to write her memoirs, she was perplexed. How to begin? Which facet of her highly complex personality should dominate? "Is it to be Chaste Madonna, or the Messalina, or the Magdalen, or the Blue Stocking?" she wondered. "Where can I find the woman of these adventures? It seems to me there was not one, but hundreds—and my soul soaring aloft, not really affected by any of them."

Speaking out at last for all women, she wrote:

> Nothing is farther from the actual truth of a personality than the hero or heroine of the average cinema play or novel. Endowed generally with all the virtues, it would be impossible for them to commit a wrong action.
>
> Nobility, courage, fortitude, etc., for *him*. Purity, sweet temper, etc., for *her*. All the meaner qualities and sins for the villain of the plot and for the 'Bad Woman,' whereas in reality we know that no one is either good or bad. We may not break the Ten Commandments, but we are certainly capable of it. Within us lurks the breaker of all laws, ready to spring out at the first real opportunity. Virtuous people are simply those who have either not been tempted sufficiently, because they live in a vegetative state, or because their purposes are so concentrated in one direction that they have not had the leisure to glance around them.

No one would ever accuse Isadora of vegetating, nor was she limited in scope. The world was a canvas on which she painted in bright bold strokes. Half-serious, half-laughing, she excused her free wheeling approach to life by claiming that she was born under the star of Aphrodite. Her mother's prenatal diet of champagne and oysters was thought to have imparted artistic impulses.

Despite aristocratic antecedents from both parents that included intimates of Washington and Lincoln, Isadora's early life was precarious. Mary Dora Gray and Joseph Duncan were divorced shortly after her birth in San Francisco on May 27, 1878. The legal action was merely a formality. Isadora's father, an itinerant real estate promoter, had disappeared with a price on his head months before. Mrs. Duncan was left to support their four children—Elizabeth, Raymond, Augustin and Isadora—by making lace and giving piano lessons.

By the time she was six, Isadora was giving lessons of her own. On her own initiative the child, who would "rather dance than eat," established a "waving school" to instill grace in the younger girls of her neighborhood. It was the beginning of a teaching tradition that would bring balance

and meaning to a tumultuous life while totally revolutioniz-
ing the art of dance.

Isadora's first conception of the rhythm of the dance was
drawn by the ceaseless motion of the waves that lashed the
seacoast close to her home. Her natural movements were
born of the back-to-nature craze that swept California in the
last decade of the 19th century. The autonomy, courage and
independence that would characterize her untrammeled life,
developed in a household where the harassed but gentle
mother was too busy to impose restrictions on her adventurous brood.

The Duncan regime was permissive in all respects. The
children peddled lace from door to door in the afternoon,
then frequently sat up until dawn reading or listening while
their dreamy-eyed mother played classical music on the battered piano. They ate and slept when they chose and moved
frequently from lodging house to lodging house—leaving a
trail of debts in their wake.

Dora Duncan supplied her children with an Irish legacy of
spirit and poetry although she was hard put to keep a roof
over their heads. At age six, Isadora astounded her teachers
by reciting William Lytle's "Antony to Cleopatra":
"I am dying, Egypt, dying!
Ebbs the crimson life-tide fast."
The school authorities were no less surprised a few months
later when Isadora, being asked to write the history of her
life, penned the following:

> When I was five we had a cottage on 23rd Street. Failing to
> pay the rent, we could not remain there but moved to 17th
> Street, and in a short time, as funds were low, the landlord
> objected, so we moved to 22nd Street, where we were not
> allowed to live peacefully but were moved to 10th Street . . .

This was merely the first paragraph of a lengthy nomadic
chronicle which she read aloud to the class in clear, dulcet
tones. The teacher interpreted the biography as a bad joke
and sent the child to the school principal, who in turn sent
for Mrs. Duncan. The poor woman, upon reading the objec-
tionable piece, burst into tears. The story was only too true.

Years later when Isadora had returned once again to San

Francisco on a nationwide tour, she made a nostalgic pilgrimage to all the homes where she had lived during those childhood years. The journey about San Francisco and East Oakland took nearly a full day in a hired chauffeur-driven limousine.

The grim realities of life about her affected the growing girl keenly. By the time she was twelve, she was well aware that the sentimental novels of the time in which married lovers lived happily ever after bore little resemblance to real life. Isadora's mother, who had been raised a Catholic, considered her abandonment and subsequent divorce to be the greatest of humiliations. Her life was lived in total celibacy, as though in atonement for the sin of divorce. Meanwhile Joseph Duncan had blithely gone on to numerous affairs and another marriage. Was this fair, their child pondered.

Isadora's voracious reading led her eventually to George Eliot's *Adam Bede*, in which a young girl brought down terrible disgrace upon herself by having a baby out of wedlock. This, coupled with the experiences that she had witnessed firsthand, triggered a strong feminist fervor in the child's heart. She promised then and there to fight against the restrictions of marriage and for the emancipation of women. Every woman should have the right to live her own life, having children or not having them according to her own wishes and not those of a confining, Puritanical society which only served to maintain women in a state of cradle to grave bondage.

A lifetime philosophy was thus forged at twelve. Isadora's audacity and candor would ultimately bring about an estrangement from her mother and the outraged disapproval of the entire world; but there would be no turning back, no hypocrisy and no compromise.

Living by her wits and charm, Isadora learned to beg early in life and continued until death. As a child, she scrounged food from butchers and grocers. Later she begged funds from a wealthy patron to go to Europe. Chance doles were her only means of support in the end. She had no sense of obligation. It was her opinion that society owed her a living regardless of how that living was to be done. Always generous herself, she expected the same unquestioning, unqualified largess from the world in general.

Mrs. Duncan informed her brood early in life that there was no Santa Claus and no God. Isadora felt it her responsibility to share this information with her peers but was sent home from school as punishment for her frankness. Lacking faith in other sources, the Duncans possessed unlimited confidence in themselves. In 1895, Dora Duncan and her four offspring reached Chicago with combined assets of $25 and some antique jewelry. Before long they were reduced to sleeping on park benches. The jewelry was pawned and they moved on to New York, where Isadora got a tiny part as a fairy dancer in "A Midsummer Night's Dream."

She was an arresting figure, tall and slender with auburn hair, a slightly tilted nose and misty blue-green eyes. Before long this beguiling free spirit was engaged to dance in the homes of New York socialites.

Reaction was mixed. Isadora's bare legs and diaphanous veils were avant-garde for the 1890's and literally laid the groundwork for today's dances and costuming. Some were enraged by her lack of concern that shapely legs could occasionally be glimpsed, for this was an era when even the "limbs" of a piano or chair were modestly pantalooned in lace. Dowagers often showed their outrage by walking out in the midst of a performance; while others, perhaps more sophisticated, were bored. For the latter, art was more than a teenage girl posturing while her sister read aloud from the *Rubiyat of Omar Khayyam* and their mother played the piano.

Having temporarily exhausted the possibilities of New York, the Duncans moved to London traveling by cattle boat on money loaned to Isadora by a socially prominent matron intrigued by the girl's promise. Once there, the family existed on penny buns and slept again on park benches. For a change of scene the twenty-year-old Isadora sauntered into a luxurious hotel, informed the clerk that her family's luggage had been lost in transit and insouciantly demanded the best accommodations. After a delicious dinner and a good night's sleep on clean sheets and downy mattresses, the five Duncans stole out unobserved.

Once again Isadora readily made her own luck when she glimpsed in a discarded newspaper that a former New York patroness of hers had taken a home in Grosvenor Square. She went to the woman, arranged a performance and in-

sisted upon payment in advance. The Duncan family dined
that night on tinned food. The remainder of the stipend was
spent on veiling for Isadora to wear when she danced to
Mendelssohn's "Spring Song." The recital was a success and
many others followed.

The British critic Titterton wrote of her at this time, "A
new idea comes into the world once in a century and today I
was the witness to one reborn."

A glittering reputation for beauty and originality preceded
Isadora to Paris where she was invited to perform at one
dazzling salon after another. Everywhere one heard members of the haute societe discussing the artistic innovations of
the shocking California girl who dared to dance barefoot.
The removal of her dancing slippers marked another innova-
tion in the natural, free-wheeling movement that characterized both Isadora's personal style and her contribution to
modern dancing. Another habit, equally controversial, that
emerged during this period was Isadora's propensity to end
each performance with a speech. The custom, which became
more and more inflammatory as the years passed, began
merely with a vow to one day open "a college of priestesses,
a school of the dance." She promised to teach an army of
young girls to renounce every sensation as she had done, so
that they might dedicate their lives to dancing.

A few months later in Budapest where Isadora had her
first love affair, she discovered within herself a taste for sensation that she would never succeed in renouncing.

Isadora's Romeo was Oscar Boregi, Hungary's leading actor, who was playing Romeo at the time. Describing the
event more than twenty-five years later, she was able to
recapture her girlish enthusiasm:

> One afternoon at a friendly gathering, over a glass of
> golden Tokay, I met two large black eyes that burned and
> glowed into mine with such ardent adoration and Hungarian
> passion that in that one look was all the meaning of the spring
> in Budapest. He was tall, of magnificent proportions, a head
> covered with luxuriant curls, black, with purple lights in
> them. Indeed he might have posed for the David of Michael-
> angelo himself. When he smiled, between his red, sensual
> lips, gleamed strong, white teeth. From our first look every
> power of attraction we possessed rushed from us in mad

embrace. From that first gaze we were already in each other's arms, and no power on earth could have prevented this.

Their initial union was less blissful than Isadora expected. "I must confess my first experience was a horrible fright," she candidly recalled, "but great pity for what he seemed to be suffering prevented me from running away from what at first was sheer torture." Boregi was ardent and Isadora eager, so ultimately their early difficulties were overcome. Rapture was theirs. Boregi felt that his whole characterization of Romeo had changed since meeting Isadora who had caused him to realize for the first time the true poignancy of Romeo's adoration.

She was to inspire many others.

Despite the shocked disapproval of Isadora's mother and sister, the enamored pair rushed off to the countryside for a few days. It was a delicious experience for Isadora to lie all night in her lover's arms. She had few thoughts beyond the moment. The romance faded slightly for her when Boregi began to talk of marriage. Assuming this event to be a foregone conclusion, he hustled her off to look at apartments. Isadora felt a strange chill at the prospect of imminent domesticity.

"What shall we do, living in Budapest?" she asked tentatively.

Boregi was surprised by the question but ready with an answer, the only answer for him. She would have a prize box at the theater every night in order to better watch him perform. Between times she would assist him with his lines. Absorbed in his new role of Mark Antony, Boregi had forgotten entirely that she, too, had a career.

Isadora clearly had not. The following day she signed a contract to tour Vienna and all the major cities of Germany. She left Budapest tearfully but with an unfaltering resolve that life contained more for her than a mere reflection of a loved one—no matter how dear.

A pattern had been established that would continue. "My life has known but two motives," she wrote years later. "They are Love and Art—and often Love has destroyed Art and often the imperious call of Art put a tragic end to Love for these two have no accord but only continual battle."

The dominating theme of her life was a struggle to maintain a balance. Isadora was totally sincere in her dedication to the dance, but lacked discipline in her personal life. Once caught in the web of emotions, all else was forgotten. Mary Desti, a close friend and confident, wrote: "Isadora could no more live without love than she could without food or music. They were as necessary to her as the breath of life and without them she sank into melancholia from which nothing could rouse her."

The Boregi interlude, brief as it was, changed the course of Isadora's life forever. Gone were the quiet evenings when she curled up after a performance with a glass of warm milk and Kant's *Critique of Pure Reason*—once a favorite means of relaxation. Now champagne, compliments and caresses were the order of the evening.

"Once I discovered that life could be a pastime as well as a tragedy, I gave myself with pagan innocence," she related twenty-five years later with enthusiasm undimmed by repetition. "Men seemed hungry for beauty, hungry for love which refreshes and inspires without fear or responsibility."

> After a performance, in my tunic with my hair crowned with roses, I was lovely. Why should this loveliness not be enjoyed? The divine pagan body, the passionate lips, the clinging arms, the sweet refreshing sleep on the shoulder of some loved one—these were joys that seemed innocent and delightful.
>
> Some people may be scandalized but I don't know why. If you have a body in which you were born to a certain amount of pain—cutting teeth, pulling out of teeth, and everyone however virtuous is subject to illness, why should you not draw from this same body the maximum of pleasure?

Isadora did not bother to list all of the men to whom she had given the maximum of pleasure. There wasn't room to in one volume, she regretfully explained. She was happy to have brought beauty and forgetfulness to so many and she hoped that each recalled the experience with pleasure and joy equal to her own.

One man who did make a special impression was Edward

Gordon Craig, a brilliant young set designer described as being "as poor in goods as he was rich in ideas." Once again it was love at first sight. They went immediately to his studio where they made love on a floor strewn with rose petals. Craig could afford no furniture.

"As flame meets flame, we burned in one bright flame," Isadora described the affair. "Here at last was my mate, my love, myself, for we were not two but one, two halves of the same soul."

The flame burned brightly for two weeks while Isadora's mother, sister and agent pounded frantically on Craig's door, pleading in vain that she come out and fulfill her contract. For a time Isadora considered the world well lost for the love of Gordon Craig. The two felt themselves to be twin souls; and, indeed, they were very much alike in creative genius and in temperament. Too much alike.

Craig resented Isadora's passion for the dancing school that she had recently founded there in Berlin. He had no interest in listening to her talk "about herself for a quarter of an hour" and disliked the fact that so many people were keenly appreciative of her original views. As many women have done, Isadora strove frantically to please and placate her man while nurturing a life of her own. Often, however, she would neglect Craig's fragile ego in an avid discussion of the principles of her school. Then, aware at last of his angry expression and stony, tight-lipped silence, she would try to make amends—"Oh, darling, have I offended you?"

"Offended? Oh, no! All women are damned nuisances and you are a damned nuisance, interfering with my work," he would snap petulantly. "Why do you want to go on stage and wave your arms about? Why don't you stay at home and sharpen my lead pencils?"

An additional complication arose when the society women who served as patronesses for Isadora's experimental dancing school learned of her open affair. Affronted by her careless confidence, they threatened to withdraw their support unless Isadora left the running of the school entirely to her sister, Elizabeth. Isadora, highly indignant, fumed. Elizabeth had her own ideas about how to conduct affairs—she simply did not make them public. It seemed clear enough that the good ladies of Berlin were not bothered by what they considered immorality but by lack of discretion. Anything was all right if only one didn't talk about it. Angrily she retaliated by tacking a special lecture on to the end of a performance. The dance symbolized the art of liberation she explained, and concluded with a favorite theme—the right of women to love and have children as they pleased.

"Of course," she admitted to the largely hostile audience, "people will respond, 'But what about the children?' Well, I could give the names of many prominent people who were born out of wedlock. It has not prevented them from obtaining fame and fortune. But leaving that, I said to myself, 'How can a woman go into this marriage contract with a man who she thinks is so mean that, in case of a quarrel, he wouldn't support his own children?'"

"If she thinks he is such a man, why should she marry him? Any intelligent woman who reads the marriage contract and then goes into it, deserves all the consequences."

An entirely different set of consequences awaited Isadora, who was at that time already pregnant with Craig's child. Obviously there was no talk of marriage. Isadora danced as long as she was able and then in the summer of 1905, she left her mother and sister in Berlin—her brothers Raymond and Augustin were now living in Paris—and went alone to a tiny seaside village in Holland. Settling down in a small villa hidden among vast sand dunes, she prepared to wait out her lonely vigil. Once again the written works of German and Greek philosophers were her chosen companions as she sat for hours alone on the beach.

From her earliest childhood, Isadora had been drawn by the restless rhythm of the waves. She had been born close to the sea and would return to it again and again in moments of crisis. "I have noticed that all the great events of my live have taken place by the sea," Isadora wrote many years later. She would one day die within sight of it.

Much time was spent in correspondence with Elizabeth, advising her on the administration of the school. Isadora also devised a series of five hundred exercises, which she believed would take her pupils from the simplest movements to the most complex. She considered it a complete compendium of the dance.

Craig paid brief, infrequent visits and was hundreds of miles away when their daughter, Deirdre, was born. Once the three were together, Isadora tried desperately to make the relationship work. Though Craig's talents as a stage manager were acknowledged, commercial success had eluded him. It was not enough for her to merely introduce the mercurial man to Eleonora Duse, the famous and temperamental Italian actress; Isadora soon found that her services as a mediator were constantly in demand.

"I see this as a small window. It cannot possibly be a large one," Eleanora Duse insisted as she stared critically at a sketch of one of his sets.

Craig could not understand Italian but sensed her negative reaction. "Tell her I won't have any damned woman interfering with my work!" he thundered in English to Isadora.

Isadora's translation was, "He says he admires your opinions and will do anything to please you." Then turning to Craig, she explained: "Eleonora says, as you are a great genius, she will not make any suggestions on your sketches, but will pass them as they are."

The duties of a pacifying interpreter took up most of Isadora's time, frequently interfering with the baby's feeding schedule. "I often suffered agonies when it was past milking time, while I explained to those artists what they did *not* say to each other!" Isadora recalled later.

Fortunately the results were worth her efforts. Duse introduced Craig as a "great genius" at the critically acclaimed opening night performance. It was a great triumph for him and a turning point in his career. For Isadora, it was a time of soul searching and decision. The financial demands of the school and the baby's birth had greatly depleted her bank account. The needs of the child and the demands of a quixotic lover had drained her energy as well. Isadora had been too long a subordinate. Now her own instinctive drives were beginning to assert themselves.

"I adored Craig," she explained later. "I loved him with all the ardor of my artist's soul, but I realized that our separation was inevitable. Yet I had arrived at that frenzied state where I could no longer live with him or without him. To live with him was to renounce my art, my personality, nay, perhaps my life, my reason itself. To live without him was to be in a continual state of depression and tortured by jealousy for which it now seemed that I had good cause. Visions of Craig in all his beauty in the arms of other women haunted me at night until I could no longer sleep. Visions of Craig explaining his art to women who gazed at him with adoring eyes—visions of Craig being pleased with other women, looking at them with that winning smile of his, taking an interest in them, caressing them—saying to himself, 'This woman pleases me. After all, Isadora is impossible.'"

A solution presented itself in the form of an offer to tour Russia. Impulsively accepting, she invited "Pim," a chance acquaintance, to accompany her. Pim was handsome, blond, debonair and probably bisexual. He traveled with eighteen trunks containing the latest in men's wear and a collection of antique snuff boxes. The capricious affair was intended for pleasure only and remained just that—Isadora thought she had had her fill of Great Love and Suffering.

The tour was a success and Isadora returned to her school in Germany minus Pim but filled with new vitality. She was doubly pleased in that she had assured Craig's continuing theatrical success by lining up a contract for him with Stanislavsky. Now she was ready to turn all her attentions to her own interests.

Although Isadora had dreamed of instructing a small army of females, she contented herself for the time being with twenty girls ranging in age from four to eight years old. To these she determined to impart some of her own idealism; "A dancer must constantly practice until her head and heart ached from the endless effort and her soul perspired," Isadora eplained to them by word and by example. A single awkward posture was monstrous, she warned. Even the people in the very last row could see that!

Dancing before a backdrop of blue curtains had become Isadora's theatrical trademark. This same color was incorporated into the decor of the practice rooms and dormitories as a keynote. She believed that creativity would flower best in a regime devoted to beauty, freedom and health. Assisted by her sister, Elizabeth, Isadora taught dancing but also strongly emphasized a thorough grounding in music and literature. Much emphasis was placed upon developing muscular coordination through acrobatics, deep breathing exercises and diet. The girls, clad in sandals and tunics, took long walks each day and their physical well-being was monitored by a doctor and dentist who were a part of the school faculty. This program was in addition to the educational routine prescribed by the German government.

Harking back to this period, Isadora later recalled, "When I was twenty-six and suddenly found myself earning large sums by my performances, I might have, like many other young women, bought pearls, diamonds and fancy clothes. It was then, however, obeying some inner voice, that I had the idea of adopting twenty poor little children, saying to myself: 'I am going to give these beings a finer life, a higher education, so that later in their turn they can spread joy and beauty about them like a glow over this sad earth.'"

Unfortunately even Isadora's relatively large earning capacity was not sufficient to maintain the school in the manner that she so earnestly desired. An appeal was made to the German government but a subsidy was denied. In an effort to raise the necessary funds for the school's continuance, Isadora returned to the United States for a nationwide tour. Uninterrupted by dalliance, the tour was both a critical and a financial success. But back in Paris a new love awaited.

One night shortly after Isadora's return to Europe a tall, handsome man came backstage to pay homage. He was Paris Eugene Singer, son of Isaac Singer, founder of the sewing machine fortune. "Lohengrin," as Isadora chose to call him, was cosmopolitan and charming, at home in all social circles and fantastically wealthy. Singer had been as much moved by Isadora's characteristic speech at the end of her performance—an impassioned plea for her school—as he was by her grace and beauty. Within a few days Isadora and her pupils had been invited by the open handed millionaire to share his seaside mansion on the French Riviera. For the first and only time in Isadora's life, romance and practicality merged. Both order and luxury prevailed. Bills were paid, obligations met; the school flourished.

Their affair was one of the most colorful of that lavish era.

A typical escapade involved a house party that started in Paris and culminated months later on a houseboat on the Nile. Shortly afterward their son, Patrick, was born. Unlike the lonely exile prior to Deirdre's birth, this pregnancy was a happy, carefree time for Isadora. Patrick, too, was born within the sight and sound of the sea but this time Isadora gave birth in a palatial mansion on the shores of the Riviera. The adoring Lohengrin remained with the expectant mother throughout and saw to it that she lacked for nothing.

Afterward the delighted father proposed marriage. Isadora remained true to her ideals. It would be stupid for an artist to marry, she protested. Her artistic life required that she make frequent tours. "Could you spend your life in the stage-box admiring me?" she asked.

Singer had no such intention. "You would not have to make tours if we were married," he answered.

"What would we do?" she asked, puzzled.

"We should spend our time in my house in London, or at my place in the country."

Isadora was unimpressed, "And then what should we do?"

"There is the yacht," he reminded her.

Isadora was still unconvinced. "But then what should we do?" she persisted doubtfully.

There was no marriage. Isadora continued to tour, although less frequently. Departing one time for an appearance in Russia, her train compartment filled with flowers from Singer, she philosophized. "It is a strange fact that when parting from a loved one, although we may be torn by the most terrible grief, we experience at the same time a curious sensation of liberation."

At home with Singer and the children, life was carefree and comfortable. The idyl continued for three years. Isadora was installed in a mansion in the fashionable Neuilly area of Paris. The house had every embellishment including gold mirrors on the walls and ceilings to reflect Isadora's varied activities. She gave lavish parties, transforming the place into a Spanish palace or a tropical garden as the mood suited her.

Of course it was too good to last. Singer was a practical

man of finance. He adored Isadora as a beautiful object but
had little sympathy for her liberal idealism. It rankled him
that because of his wealth he was blamed for all the social
injustices of the world by his darling. Isadora's lengthy
tirades on art and freedom were often at best boring, at worst
disturbing. The more possessive he became, the more she
drew away.

Delightful and convenient as life with Singer must have
been for Isadora, her children and dancing pupils, it seems
likely that an ordered, disciplined existence was simply beyond the dancer's capacity. However attractive, a cage remained a cage; a possessive man became a keeper. A permanent alliance with one individual must invariably prove too
restrictive for her fiercely independent nature. Isadora
would belong to herself at whatever the cost to convention or
creature comforts.

The Singer saga ended abruptly when "Lohengrin" appeared unexpectedly and found Isadora making love with a
guest. Though things were never the same between them,
Singer remained her true friend to the end. She would have
need of his strength and loyalty within the year.

At the time of their separation Isadora felt more liberated
than repentant. Her attempts at domesticity had been abortive. Could art and life ever be reconciled, she wondered. It
seemed to her that extra barriers were placed before a
woman desiring to be an artist. She saw art as a hard task-
master who demanded everything, yet a woman in love was
expected to give up everything to accommodate to love.
Even her own anatomy was an enemy, demanding that she
sacrifice art to re-create life.

Isadora's joy in her renewed autonomy was shattered with
macabre finality in the spring of 1913 when her two children
were drowned in a runaway car. The tragedy occurred when
the chauffeur got out, without braking the car, to crank the
motor into action. He was tossed to one side as the car slid
down a grassy embankment and plunged into the Seine.
Despite repeated efforts to save them, Deirdre, Patrick and
their nurse were drowned in the muddy river bottom.

Singer came immediately to share Isadora's grief and to
offer support and solace. Soon the whole street in which she

lived was filled with flowers—there was no longer room left within the house. Strangers who had never known the children or their mother sought to express their sympathy with more floral offerings. The students from the Ecole des Beaux Arts bought every white flower in Paris and during the night tied these to the trees and bushes in Isadora's garden. Claude Debussy came to offer his condolences. After standing for a time in anguished silence before the grieving mother, he went to the piano. In a moment he was improvising music that personified their sadness. It was his immortal *Danse Macabre.*

Gordon Craig responded immediately, writing from Florence where he was then living. It was a letter that Isadora would cherish until her own tragic death. Craig wrote, in part:

> Isadora dear—I never shall be able to say anything to you. It is a mysterious thing but when I begin to think of you or speak to you I feel as though it was as unnecessary as if I should speak to myself. This feeling grows. . . .
>
> My life as yours has been strange—you are strange—but not to me. And my darling I know how you can suffer and not show more than a smile. I know your weakness which is that of a dear little fool—for I, a big fool, have looked at you. I know your strength too—for I who can taste strength have seen all yours. My heart has broken to see your weakness. Large chips (you couldn't have noticed them, for I as you, will never show them). My heart has often shaken with terror to see your strength. For my heart and your heart are one heart and an utterly incomprehensible thing it is. I want to be with you—and it was only to say that I write so much. And as I am with you, being you, what more is there to be said. Let us not be sorry for anything—or where shall we begin. You and I are lonely—only that. And no matter how many came—or shall come—you and I must be lonely—our secret. I kiss your heart.

Isadora's own initial grief was expressed by executing a death dance dedicated to her children. To those who were shocked by this seemingly egotistical display, she explained that the special dance was her way of mourning. She was composed at the funeral. "No tears," she admonished. "They never knew sorrow. We must not be sorrowful today.

I want to be brave enough to make death beautiful and to help all other mothers of the world who have lost their babies."

Brave words, yet the rest of Isadora's life was spent in frantic, futile efforts to forget her crushing grief.

"Do not seek happiness again," her dear friend, Eleonora Duse advised her when she saw Isadora drifting toward another affair. "You have on your brow the mark of the great unhappy ones of the earth. Do not tempt fate again."

The warning went unheeded. Isadora was to have another baby, who died only a few minutes after birth. The father was a young Italian sculptor, already engaged to another, who soon drifted out of Isadora's life forever.

For the distraught Isadora it was as though her original loss had been re-enacted with all its sorrow; only now hope, too, seemed to have disappeared. The transitory alliance with the young man had been solely for the purpose of having another child—a child that she fervently hoped would be a reincarnation of Deirdre or Patrick. Now this child also had been taken from her.

As Paris rushed to mobilize for World War I, Isadora lay for weeks sunk in a black desolation from which there seemed no escape. Then one day she rose, made arrangements for her dancing students to be sent to the United States, and ordered her home transformed into a hospital to house the wounded.

Following her pupils to New York, Isadora took up briefly with Singer. With his characteristic generosity, he engaged the Metropolitan Opera House for her to dance in and then presented his wayward love with a magnificent diamond necklace. After the performance she was the life of the party he gave in her honor, dancing an impassioned tango with a well known playboy. Jealously Singer wrenched Isadora from her partner's arms, then smashed china and glassware in his fury. This was merely one more scandal for Isadora, but for Singer it marked the end of any lingering affection. Only compassion and bittersweet memories remained of his once great love for her.

Isadora's enthusiastic attempts to establish municipal dance schools in New York and San Francisco met with no civic response. While visiting the latter city on tour, Isadora called on her mother who had returned to live there when Deirdre was born. The two had lunch at the famous Cliff House over looking the stormy Pacific. Catching a glimpse of their faces reflected in a mirror, Isadora was momentarily shocked. Dora Duncan's appearance was old and careworn, the expression on her own face was one of sadness. Could these be the same two adventurous spirits who had set out nearly twenty-two years before in search of fame and fortune? Both had been found, she reasoned, why was the ultimate result so tragic? Perhaps so-called happiness simply did not exist in any lasting form; there were only peak moments of joy to be savored to the utmost. She shrugged philosophically, recognizing better than most the value of those rare moments. Isadora was never one to shrink from experience, realizing almost from the beginning that if life didn't come between loved ones—death surely would.

Both romance and art were at a temporary standstill for Isadora in 1921 when she received a telegram from the Soviet Government, a place considered to be a veritable hell by most Americans and Europeans. It read:

"The Russian Government alone can understand you. Come to us: we will make your School."

She needed no other encouragement. Despite the horrified objections of her friends and lovers who had heard terrifying tales of the barbaric new regime, Isadora was soon bound for Moscow. Just before leaving, she capriciously consulted a fortune teller, who prophesied: "You are bound on a long journey. You will have many strange experiences. You will have troubles. You will marry——"

Isadora's amused laughter cut her short. Marriage was inconceivable. "Wait and see," the woman predicted complacently.

Shortly after her arrival, Isadora was greeted by Ilya Schneider, a young writer and dance critic employed in the People's Commissariat for Foreign Affairs. Schneider would recall their shared experiences in a biography, *Isadora Duncan, the Russian Years*. Writing nearly fifty years later of their first meeting, he said, "To me, Isadora Duncan was the personification of extraordinary femininity, grace, poetry, the like of which it was scarcely to be expected that I would ever see. Now I had an unexpected impression: she looked big and monumental, her head set proudly on a regal neck and covered with the reddish copper of smooth, thick short hair. Before me sat a great artist, the reformer of the art of the dance, the 'Queen of Gesture,' as she was called, of whom Auguste Rodin had said that 'she took the force from nature which did not go under the name of talent, but genius.'"

Though Schneider threw himself into the task of helping her to establish the school, there were numerous setbacks. The fledgling communist government was no more willing to release funds than its capitalist counterparts. Once again Isadora was expected to underwrite most of the costs herself. This was further complicated by the fact that she had brought almost no money with her to Russia. In her naivete, Isadora had assumed that everything would be free in a communist paradise.

A small trickle of money was raised through a series of rigorous tours into the hinterlands where Isadora lived and danced under the most primitive conditions. There were many deprivations and several times Isadora and her accompanist were stranded in remote areas. Once totally without funds or credit, they went three days without food. Somehow she found the strength and enthusiasm to continue.

Back in Moscow those days of incredible hardship were soon forgotten. Isadora was in love again, this time with Sergei Essenine, the peasant Poet Laureate of the new regime. Though Isadora spoke only pidgin Russian and Essenine no English whatsoever, they were irresistibly drawn to one another at first meeting.

At a party given in the studio of a mutual friend the two sat together all night long. Isadora reclined on a sofa, stroking the golden hair of Essenine who sat adoringly at her feet reciting his poetry. It is unlikely that she understood a word, nor could she know then that this was one of the hooligan poet's rare docile moments. At four in the morning, they left the remnants of the party and went to Isadora's apartment. It was the beginning of a stormy union that only death could sever.

Though Sergei's idea of entertainment was running nude

through the streets and smashing furniture, Isadora was for a time undaunted. She was overwhelmed as much by his emerging genius as by his youthful passion. Her questing soul sought fulfillment in both. She chose to ignore his sudden fits of madness along with the disparity in their ages. He was twenty-seven, she forty-four.

"I resent the conclusion formed by so many women that after the age of forty, a dignified life should exclude all love making," she explained in her memoirs. "Ah, how wrong this is! How mysterious it is to feel the life of the body all through this weird journey on earth."

"First, the timid shrinking body of the young girl I was and then the change to hearty Amazon. Then the bacchante drenched with wine and growing and expanding the soft flesh."

Isadora and Essenine surprised everyone including themselves by marrying. The school needed money that Isadora felt could best be raised by a tour of the United States. She could not bear the thought of separation from her young lover—perhaps realizing that their days together would not be many—and knowing that he would never be allowed entry into the United States on his own, marriage seemed the only solution.

Even with the legal amenities adhered to, the couple was detained on Ellis Island. Isadora's eloquent commentaries on the Bolshevik cause relayed 'round the world via headlines had not endeared her to the folks back home. She was interrogated for hours; Essenine was forced to sign a statement promising not to sing the Soviet anthem.

Undaunted by her cool reception, Isadora had hardly set foot on American soil before she began expounding on the advantages of a more equalitarian regime. Once her enthusiasm for a cause was ignited, it was simply impossible for her to maintain any sense of discretion. "You don't know what beauty is," she accused a cool Bostonian audience. Then, tearing open her tunic, she bared one of her breasts, exclaiming, "This is beauty!"

Later she attempted to explain, "Why should I care what part of my body I reveal? Is not all body and soul an instrument through which the artist expresses his inner measure of beauty?"

She denied vehemently that either she or Essenine were interested in spreading propaganda. Their concern was for the starving children of Russia, not the country's politics. "Sergei is not a politician," she insisted, "he is a genius."

Sergei's genius unfortunately did not extend to personal relationships. The luxury that now surrounded the former peasant seemed to inflame him. He was constantly drunk and on one occasion ripped off his wife's gown. The tour was a debacle and once again Paris Singer came to Isadora's rescue. It was he who provided the return passage for the newlyweds.

Before sailing back to Europe on the *S.S. George Washington,* Isadora made one last effort to clarify her position. "I am not an anarchist or a Bolshevik," she told assembled reporters. "My husband and I are revolutionists. All geniuses worthy of the name are. Every artist has to be one to make a mark in the world today."

In an effort to nurture Essenine's genius which was endangered by his own frequent debaucheries, Isadora tried in every way to subordinate herself. "Forget that I'm the great artist," she pleaded to her lifelong friend, Mary Desti. "I'm just a nice, intelligent person who appreciates the great genius of Sergei Essenine. He is the artist; he, the great poet." Despite her efforts the tormented poet's drinking increased. Isadora's well intentioned blend of mothering, cajoling and passion failed because it only served to underscore his growing dependency upon her. There were numerous violent quarrels, angry partings and sorrowful reunions.

The following year Essenine committed suicide in the same Petrograd hotel room where he and Isadora had stayed during the early, blissful days of their union. Her name was found written in his blood.

Isadora wound up in Nice where she was able to obtain sustenance from her brother, Raymond. Sometimes she sat staring out at the sea with tears streaming down her face, but far more often there were happy hours of gaiety and flirtation. Isadora was invariably buoyant, rarely willing to concede defeat even momentarily.

"I like young men and potatoes," she quipped and spent what little money she had on both.

Singer was staying at his villa close by and frequently

aided her financially. On the final occasion she said, "I am beginning to be a great nuisance; nothing can be done about me and I can no more change my habits than a leopard his spots." She gave several performances that were critical if not financial successes. Isadora still had fond hopes of starting a new dancing school in Nice.

She was in fine spirits on September 14, 1927, when fate once again seemed to take charge of an automobile. Attracted by a red sports car and its salesman, a young flying ace, she arranged to have both come by for inspection.

When the man drove up to the bar where she waited with friends, Isadora gayly flung a scarlet scarf about her head and shoulders. Her eyes sparkled, her face was flushed with excitement, she was elated, ready as always for a new adventure. "Good-by, I'm on my way to glory," she cried, looking back over her shoulder as the handsome driver helped her into the low two-seated sports car.

Isadora's life ended as dramatically as it had been lived. Her neck was broken by her own colorful scarf which had caught in the rear wheel of the racing car.

One last time Paris Singer came forward to help. All the funeral arrangements were made by him. More than 10,000 persons attended the event. News of Isadora's death was flashed around the world and thousands of friends sent flowers.

Many pronouncements were made about her, but perhaps the truest was expressed by Sol Hurok, the impressario who had managed her turbulent tour only a few years before:

"I knew that Isadora loved life as perhaps no human being has ever loved it; that she was the embodiment of life, generous, zestful life, to those who knew and loved her.

"Because of her, women are freed from their corsets and conventions. The bodies of little children are freed. She brought sunlight and fresh air into the lives of all of us, she cut the bonds of spirit as well as flesh."

4

Helena Blavatsky

Mother of Mysticism

"Nobody's perfect," the cliche reminds us. But what about high priestesses, theologians, gurus and other cult leaders? Are they immune from human imperfection? Who are they? *What* are they? And where do they come from?

Is an infant mystic somehow divine—different from other babies—better, wiser, kinder? Helena Blavatsky, who introduced the study of the occult to the Western world, appears to have displayed the antithesis of the gentler virtues. Almost from the moment of birth on August 12, 1831, at Ekaterinoslav in the Ukraine, Helena demonstrated a wayward courage and an insatiable desire to establish and maintain her own individuality. Throughout the vicissitudes of her tempestuous and highly controversial life, she would always remain a law unto herself.

An aunt once wrote of Helena, "From her earliest childhood she was unlike any other person. Very lively and highly gifted, she was full of humor and of the most remarkable daring. Helena's unaccountable attraction to—and fear of—the dead, her passionate love and curiosity for everything unknown, mysterious, weird and fantastical ought to have warned us that she was an exceptional creature."

This "exceptional creature" would ultimately bring a new dimension to Western thought, a challenging alternative to traditional religious dogma. By introducing the Eastern doctrine of reincarnation to the West, Helena brought solace to many by explaining the inequalities of present life, interpreting the seemingly haphazard distribution of happiness and

misery, wisdom and ignorance. Her concept of *karma* with its inevitable chain of cause and effect on future existences still offers people peace, comfort and acceptance—qualities that Helena would never possess herself.

Helena's mother, Helene Andreyevna Fadeef, the daughter of a Russian princess, was married at sixteen to Colonel Peter von Hahn, a dashing cavalry officer in the Russian Army. Quickly bored by garrison life, she sought release from the confines of domesticity by establishing herself as a writer. Madame Hahn's novels—cynical tales in which the female characters invariably emerged as victims—were so well received that she early won the accolade, "Russia's George Sand."

To escape the boredom of the army post and perhaps to assume control of her own life, Madame Hahn made numerous visits to Saint Petersburg where she was much admired in literary circles. But beauty, talent and charm could not protect her from the hazards of being a woman in the 19th century. At twenty-eight, Helene Hahn had written twelve novels, borne two daughters—and died giving birth to a son.

Among her last words were, "Ah well, perhaps it is best

that I am dying so at least I shall be spared seeing what befalls Helena! Of one thing I am certain, her life will not be that of other women and she will have much to suffer."

Prophetic as Madame Hahn's words later proved to be, Helena's early years seem to have been guided by friendly forces. At thirteen, while riding horseback, her mount became frightened and bolted. The child was unseated; but, instead of being thrown, felt herself supported by unseen hands until the horse finally came to a halt. She credited the spectral form of a giant Hindu wearing a white turban with this mysterious intervention. Helena claimed to have been aware of his presence since earliest childhood and called him her "Protector." Unfortunately, he was powerless to protect the girl from her own headstrong temperament. It was enough to forbid her doing a thing to cause her to do it. At fifteen she still rode on a man's saddle as she had at age ten—defying all the traditions of her time.

Helena's arrogance softened briefly when while at her grandparents' estate in Tiflis she fell deeply in love with Prince Alexander Galitsin, a cousin of the viceroy's. For a time the handsome prince was constantly at her family's home in the capital city of Georgia. He was avidly interested in the occult and the study of magic and had a decided influence on the course of Helena's life. At the same time he may have found her attempts to influence him more than he cared to accept. Whatever the reason, Prince Galitsin broke their engagement and hurriedly left Tiflis.

Her ego was painfully wounded and Helena lashed out angrily, "There is nothing of the woman in me. If a man dares to speak to me of love I would have him shot like a dog who bit me." She decided that the structured pomp of Czarist society was not for her. When her family insisted that she attend the viceroy's ball, an appearance considered obligatory, Helena angrily refused.

"I hate 'society' and the so-called 'world' and I hate hypocrisy," she ranted. Unimpressed, her grandfather sent word that if necessary he would have the maids dress her by force. "I then deliberately plunged my foot and leg into a kettle of boiling water and held it there till nearly boiled raw," Helena recalled years later, admitting, "Of course, I scalded it horribly and remained at home for six months."

It was during this period of convalescence that a servant chided Helena for her sharp tongue, "Even old General Nikifor Blavatsky, who you laughed at for being so ugly, wouldn't have you for a wife."

Still smarting from Galitsin's rebuff, Helena jumped at the challenge without considering the consequences. Three days later she had induced the general, vice-governor of the province of Erivan in Transcaucasia, to propose and was engaged to be married. As soon as she was betrothed she realized her mistake but the deed could not be undone. Helena's beloved father was 4,000 miles away commanding his Cossack regiment and the rest of the family was unwilling to risk a scandal by offending Blavatsky. Perhaps, too, Helena's grandparents were delighted to be rid of the willful girl.

One month short of her seventeenth birthday, Helena was married to a man three times her age. If the precocious teenager consoled herself with the idea that she would have more freedom as a married woman she was speedily disillusioned. Shortly afterward, Helena wrote, "Woman finds her happiness in the acquisition of supernatural powers. Love is but a vile dream, a nightmare." It seems doubtful that much love was involved—certainly not on her part.

After a stormy three month honeymoon, Helena managed to elude the Cossack bodyguards assigned her and escape over the mountains on horseback to her family's home in Tiflis. Just how sorry the general was to see his incorrigible bride go is questionable, but there's little doubt of her grandfather's chagrin at having her back. Hastily, he made plans to ship her off to her father who was residing in Saint Petersburg. Entrusting her to a maid and three male servants, the old man waved an enthusiastic farewell.

Colonel Hahn traveled 2,000 miles to Odessa where a rendezvous had been arranged only to find that his errant daughter had once again given her retainers the slip. Only a few hours before his arrival, she had eloped with the captain of an English ship bound for Constantinople. The affair—if short-lived—served its purpose. Helena disembarked in Turkey a free agent far removed from parental authority. However, she was also far removed from the vast wealth and luxury, the pampering and protection that she had taken for granted since birth. But she was apparently undismayed by this sudden transition, and parlayed her equestrian skill into an exciting if unorthodox career in the circus.

A few months later while riding bareback on a white horse in a Turkish circus, she caught the eye of Agardi Metrovitch, a popular opera star. Although the few extant portraits of Helena do not act as evidence she apparently possessed great appeal. Metrovitch eagerly introduced himself to Helena and returned night after night until he persuaded her to leave the circus and travel with him on his singing tour of the capitals of Europe. Helena went with him but maintained her own identity throughout her travels in a manner reminiscent of her mother. Her astonished grandparents learned via the newspapers that Helena was in turn giving pianoforte concerts in London, managing the royal choir in the court of King Milan of Serbia, and assisting the celebrated medium, Daniel Home, in Paris.

Metrovitch communicated his activities to her grandparents on a more personal level. In an impulsive burst of affection, he wrote identifying himself as Helena's husband—despite the fact that she was still legally bound to Blavatsky. He signed himself with winsome insouciance, "Grandson."

A few years later Grandfather Fadeef, who was director of the Russian Department of State Lands in the Caucasus, and his wife, the princess, received a letter from another grandson, this time an Englishman. Writing from the United States, this neo-relative also claimed to have married Helena and brought her to America with him on a business trip.

In the early 1850s Helena found still another admirer. He was Albert Rawson, who had encountered the intrepid young woman in Cairo. She was a "charming young widow," he recalled many years later, who "could fascinate the most indifferent man in a single interview." Rawson was no dullard himself and his standards were high. An author, artist and world traveler, he possessed among many honors an LL.D from Oxford University. Though an American, he had somehow managed to disguise himself as a Mohammedan divinity student in order to make the sacred pilgrimage

to Mecca. Now he was more than eager to share his knowledge of the Near East with this intriguing woman whom he
described as combining "femininity and masculine willful-
ness."

Helena was an apt pupil. Mounted on camels, the two
rode out to the Pyramids, spending three nights in their
shadow. Donning the clothes of Moslem dandies, they explored bazaars and visited Egyptian snake charmers. Helena
was eager to show off her learning. The Countess Kissalev,
an old family friend whom she'd chanced to meet in Cairo,
was her unfortunate subject. "I've solved the mysteries of
Egypt," Helena exclaimed with childlike glee and then
pulled a live serpent from a bag she had concealed in the
folds of her skirt. The poor countess shrieked in horror as the
snake slithered about her luxurious suite in Shepherd's
Hotel.

A few days later when the countess was watching the sun
set across the desert with Rawson and Helena, she found the
latter in a more introspective mood. "I have before me forty
years in which to build a more enduring fame than that of
the builder of the Great Pyramid, for who was he anyway?
Only a name, an oppressor of his fellow men," Helena announced. "I will bless mankind by freeing them from their
mental bondage. I know I was intended to do a great work."

Her words proved to be prophetic. Suddenly, ten years
after her departure, Helena returned to her family as
abruptly as she had left. Her sister, Vera, recalled in her
memoirs that the prodigal appeared unexpectedly in the
midst of a family wedding feast. "We embraced each other,
overcome with joy, forgetting for the moment the strange-
ness of the event," she wrote. "That very evening I was
convinced that my sister had acquired strange powers. She
was constantly surrounded, awake or asleep, with mysterious movements, strange sounds, little taps which came from
all sides—from the furniture, from the window-panes, from
the ceiling, from the floor, from the walls. They were very
distinct and seemed intelligent into the bargain; they tapped
three times for 'yes,' twice for 'no.'"

Family friends flocked to view the notorious visitor and to
gape at the mysterious phenomena that surrounded her.

"Mistrust and irony were often shown," Sister Vera admitted, "but Helena bore it all coolly and patiently. It was her usual habit to sit very quietly and quite unconcerned on the sofa, or in the armchair, engaged in some embroidery, and apparently without the slightest interest or active part in the hubbub which she produced around herself. And the hubbub was great indeed. One of the guests would be reciting the alphabet; another putting down the answers received, while the mission of the rest was to offer mental questions which were always and promptly answered." (Apparently by way of the "tapping" spirits.)

To dispel some of the skepticism, Helena allowed herself to be "subjected to the most stupid demands," according to Vera. "She was searched, her hands and feet tied with string."

Helena was revenged a week or so later when an elegant lady caller asked what was the best conductor for the production of "raps." "Could they be done anywhere?" she asked. The answer, spelled out in a series of taps, was the word, "gold," followed by, "we will prove it to you immediately." Vera recalled that the woman smiled expectantly and then suddenly paled, jumped from her chair, covering her mouth with a bejeweled hand. "Her face was convulsed with fear and astonishment. Why? Because she had felt the raps in her mouth, as she confessed later on. Those present looked at each other significantly. Previous even to her own confession all had understood that the lady had felt a violent commotion, raps in the gold of her artificial teeth."

A family member who shared little of Vera's enthusiasm regarding Helena was their cousin, Count Sergei Witte, who later served his country as acting Prime Minister and represented Russia during peace negotiations with Japan in 1904 conducted at Portsmouth, New Hampshire.

Witte, writing in his memoirs, recalls Helena at the time of her homecoming. "Her face, apparently once of great beauty, bore all traces of a tempestuous and passionate life, and her form was marred by an early obesity. She paid scant attention to her appearance, and preferred loose mourning dresses to more elaborate apparel. But her eyes were extraordinary. She had enormous azure-colored eyes and when she spoke with animation, they sparkled in a fashion which is altogether indescribable. Never in my life have I seen anything like that pair of eyes."

Despite Count Witte's unflattering analysis regarding Helena's appearance, he was forced to admit that she held court nightly, totally captivating the jaded, mostly male, aristocracy with her mediumistic demonstrations. Wives and sisters usually remained at home, nursing their outraged virtue and resentment toward the notorious Helena.

At her grandfather's insistence, there was a brief reconciliation with General Blavatsky. "But," wrote Witte, "it was not given to Helena to walk in the paths of righteousness for any length of time." One day shortly thereafter Helena encountered her former lover, Agardi Metrovitch, who was performing in Tiflis. Their old attraction flared again and they ran off together. Unfortunately Metrovich's career was slipping and it remained for Helena to augment their income by operating an ink factory in Odessa and sometime later an artificial flower shop in Kiev.

Even Witte was impressed by "the extraordinary facility with which she acquired skill and knowledge of the most varied description. Her abilities in this respect verged on the uncanny." (Uncanny to Witte, perhaps, Helena believed that her Hindu "Protector" was always at her side guiding and advising.) But persecution by scandalized Russian society, which insisted upon discretion if not chastity, drove Metrovitch and Helena to Italy, where their son, Youry, was born.

The episode ended with the death of the boy, a hopeless cripple, a few years later. Helena abandoned what was apparently her one period of domesticity and threw herself into the battle for the unification of Italy; she joined the army. Fighting as a volunteer under the Italian hero, Garibaldi, Helena sustained a stab wound under the heart, an arm broken in two places by sabre strokes and musket shots in the shoulder and leg. Following her convalescence and remarkable recovery Helena and Metrovitch sailed for Egypt where Metrovitch hoped to join a touring Italian opera company. On June 21, 1871, their ship, the *S.S. Eumonia*, which was carrying a cargo of gun powder, blew up. Of four hundred passengers, only seventeen survived. Helena but not Metrovich was among them.

Rescued with no possessions but the clothes on her back, Helena was put ashore in Alexandria. A few months short of her fortieth birthday, she had lost family, husband, child, lover. She was totally alone and without prospects.

How or where Helena was able to obtain funds to go to Cairo is unknown but once there she succeeded in establishing herself as a medium of note. This was a difficult, soul-shattering period. Desperate as she was to sustain herself, Helena became critical of the practice of spiritualism, which she believed had a demoralizing effect upon mediums. She removed herself from the beggarly group of charlatans about her who were cannily augmenting their meager talents with show tricks, and organized a research group, the *Societe Spirite*. But good intentions and a grandiose name could not protect her from fraud even within the ranks of the Societe.

Helena complained bitterly in a letter to a wealthy relative living in Paris. Most of her associates she said, were merely part-time mediums and full-time adventurers who were camp-following the engineers then engaged in constructing the Suez Canal. "They drink like fishes, steal my money and cheat the patrons," she lamented. The response was boat fare to Paris.

At this point Helena made a last attempt to lead a conventional life under the protection of her wealthy and highly respected family. But it was no use. Though she barely had money enough to pay for steerage passage, Helena was soon again in motion. On July 7, 1873, twenty-five years after her marriage to Nikifor Blavatsky, she landed in New York City. She was determined to dig in and make a stand, to grasp the world by its ears and climb on top. She did not dare fail. Helena was well aware that the hoyden charm of her youth had faded long ago; and she had seen firsthand what became of the women like herself who lived by their wits but let the years go by without achieving lasting recognition and prominence.

She was forty-three years old. Her blue eyes were huge and round, her fair hair short and crinkled like a mature Little Orphan Annie. Her body, though corpulent, had a heroic, larger than life appearance. Helena had crossed the Rockies by covered wagon, explored the jungles of Africa and climbed the Andes. At voodoo rites in the West Indies, from Tibetan monks, Indian shamans, African witch doctors, Hindu holy men and Persian sorcers, she had learned strange secrets. These she yearned to share with the world.

Unfortunately the world was not quite ready to receive them yet. For a time the granddaughter of a princess found work in a sweatshop. She lived in one of New York's first tenement houses, on the lower east side. The place was designated a "Home for Working Women" and it housed sixty-five occupants, mostly unskilled.

An exception was Elizabeth Holt, a young school teacher who later wrote of the circumstances that had brought them together. "There were no women in business," she recalled. "A few were beginning to be heard clamoring for their 'rights'; but the women who had to go out into the world to earn a living were telegraphers, sewers of various kinds and workers at small trades which paid very badly. The typewriter had not yet been invented. The house was unique and a product of that particular era. It was hard then for respectable women workers of small means to find a fitting place in which to live. Being a co-operative family, we all knew one another familiarly and kept a room next to the street door as a common sitting-room or office."

It was here that Helena spent much of her time, but rarely alone. Ms. Holt describes her as "a magnet powerful enough to draw round her everyone who could possibly come. I saw her day after day, sitting there rolling her cigarettes and smoking incessantly. She had a conspicuous tobacco pouch, the head of some fur-bearing animal, which she wore about her neck. I think she must have been taller than she looked, she was so broad. Her whole appearance conveyed the idea of power. I read somewhere lately an account of an interview with Stalin. The writer said when you entered the room you felt as if there was a powerful dynamo working. You felt something like that when you were near her."

Despite her fascination, Ms. Holt was disapproving. "I never looked upon Madame as an ethical teacher," she wrote primly. "For one thing, she was too excitable. When things went wrong with her, she could express her opinion about them with a vigor which was very disturbing." Yet Elizabeth Holt was willing to temporize, "I would say that I never saw her angry with any person or thing at close range. Her objections had an impersonality about them . . . In mental or physical dilemma, you would instinctively appeal to her, for you felt her fearlessness, her unconventionality, her great wisdom and wide experience and hearty good will—her sympathy with the underdog."

One day Helena read in the *New York Graphic* of a series of seances being held in an obscure Vermont farmhouse. The articles, written by a Colonel Henry Olcott, were sold out almost as fast as they were written, she noticed. Both the spiritualistic phenomena and the reporter—a noted lawyer and distinguished Civil War hero as well as the country's foremost authority on spiritualism—intrigued her. Audaciously, she determined to risk her remaining funds on a train ticket.

On October 14, 1874, Helena appeared at the Eddy farm in Chittenden, Vermont. She was herself a spiritualist, she explained, having devoted her life to defending honest mediums from unjust charges. In fact, she confided to William and Horatio Eddy—the two farmers who had attracted the unexplained phenomena—she had forsaken an easy life "amongst a civilized society" to wander the earth "for the sake of the blessed truths of spiritualism."

With Colonel Olcott she was more coy. Pretending not to recognize him she paused before him and chattered artlessly, "I hesitated before coming here because I was afraid of meeting that Colonel Olcott."

"Why should you be afraid of him, Madame?"

"Oh! because I fear that he might write about me in his paper."

A married man of forty-two, Olcott was a surprisingly easy victim. He was flattered by her credulity and charmed by her confusion. Then, as all sorts of exotic phenomena began to appear about her he became fascinated. It was the beginning of a relationship that endured until her death.

With Helena's arrival the whole character of the seances changed. The grim Eddy brothers had produced a series of

American Indian spirits—*Bright Star, Honto* and *Santum*—who called out routine messages to the audience from a variety of dead relatives. Suddenly spiritual reminders of Helena's bizarre past appeared. Though only she could identify them, everyone in the audience saw the apparitions.

The first arrival Helena recognized immediately as Michalko, a Georgian servant, who obligingly played a Circassian dance at her request. Colonel Olcott's newspaper accounts describe "a person of middle height, well shaped, dressed in Georgian jacket with loose sleeves and long pointed oversleeves, an outer long coat, baggy trousers, leggings of yellow leather and a white skull-cap or fez with a tassel."

Next appeared Hassan Agha, who Helena introduced as a wealthy Tiflis merchant. Olcott dutifully recorded that this spirit was outfitted in "a long yellowish coat, Turkish trousers, a *bishmet* or vest, and a black cap covered with the national *bashlik* or hood, with its long tasseled ends thrown over each shoulder."

The awestruck farmers barely had a chance to digest these spectral guests before even more spectacular spirits appeared on the horizon. Helena easily identified a Kurd warrior who had once saved her life, a former Tartar servant who bowed low and said, *"Tchock yachtchi,"* (which she explained meant, "All right"), an African juju wearing a fancy headdress, and a distinguished gentleman wearing the Cross of Saint Anne who introduced himself to the group as her uncle.

In reporting the events to the world via the *New York Graphic*, Olcott assured his readers, "It will be seen that a lady of such social position would be incapable of entering into a vulgar conspiracy with any private trickster to deceive the public." It was, indeed, difficult to explain away. Hundreds of people had witnessed the phenomena and though every attempt was made to account for the apparitions in terms of earthly realities, no one succeeded. The spirits, it seemed, had literally appeared out of nowhere. The Eddy farmhouse was merely a farmhouse—no trap doors, sliding panels or false doors were uncovered.

Helena made a triumphant exit from Chittenden, Colonel

Olcott in tow. He was a willing captive, instantly dazzled by her flamboyant charms. Recalling their meeting, he wrote years later, "My eye was first attracted by a scarlet Garibaldian shirt she wore, as a vivid contrast with the dull colors around. Her hair was then a thick blond mop, worn shorter than the shoulders, and it stood out from her head, silken-soft and crinkled to the roots like the fleece of a Cotswold ewe. This and the red shirt were what struck my attention before I took in the picture of her features. It was a massive Calmuck face, contrasting in its suggestion of power, culture and imperiousness as strangely with the commonplace visages about the room as her red garment did with the gray and white tones of the walls and woodwork and the dull costumes of the rest of the guests."

"Good gracious!" he recalled exclaiming to a companion, "look at that specimen, will you." Spiritually speaking, at least, the Colonel and Blavatsky seemed made for each other. Olcott had been an associate editor of the *New York Tribune* sent abroad at twenty-six to study European farming methods. He later married the daughter of a minister and fathered three sons. After distinguishing himself in the Civil War, Henry Olcott was appointed commissioner and earned a national commendation for uncovering corruption in the military. Following this Olcott was one of three men appointed to investigate the extent of the Lincoln assassination conspiracy. He was later admitted to the bar and maintained a law office in New York, but preferred to retain his newspaper contacts with an occasional front page story. He covered such important general interest events as the hanging of John Brown but specialized in writing about spiritualism.

Though Olcott and Helena ultimately took up residence together, both stoutly maintained that their relationship was platonic. It was a "chumship," they agreed. He called her "Jack" and she referred to him unaccountably as "Mahoney." "Each of us," wrote Olcott by way of explanation, "felt as if we were of the same social world, cosmopolitans, free-thinkers and in closer touch (with each other) than with the rest of the company. It was the voice of common sympathy with the higher occult side of man and nature; the attraction of soul to soul, not sex to sex." So platonic was their relationship that shortly after their meeting at the Eddy home, Helena confided to Olcott that her old wound under the heart was opening up. Pulling aside her red shirt and other garments, she revealed the troublesome stiletto stab plus her other battle scars. Although Olcott recounted the experience at length in his memoirs, with a detailed list of the nature and location of Helena's many injuries, he neglected to mention what followed the disclosure.

Not long after the encounter at the Eddy farmhouse, Olcott's employer, the *Graphic* editor, decided to do a feature article about her. "She is handsome," he wrote, "with full voluptuous figure, large eyes, well-formed nose and rich sensuous mouth and chin. She dresses with remarkable elegance and her clothing is redolent of some subtle and delicious perfume which she had gathered in her wanderings in the Far East . . ."

Not surprisingly, Helena created quite a stir around the *Graphic* city room. "Do you fellows smoke here," she asked the assembled group of curious and admiring men.

"I don't," replied her interviewer.

"Oh, you mean fellow!"

"But the others do, and you can smoke if you wish."

"All we Russian ladies like our cigarette," Helena explained as she took out her cigarette papers and some Turkish tobacco, deftly rolling an elegant little cigarette. "Why, did you know poor Queen Victoria is nearly frightened into fits because her Russian daughter-in-law smokes?"

Puffing steadily, she encapsulated a few events in her colorful past, all the while blowing smoke through her "beautiful nostrils." To a woman reporter, she referred to herself as a widow despite the fact that Blavatsky, the balding general (that she had once called a plumeless raven), was still very much alive. (He would outlive her.) "Married!" she exclaimed in an indignant response to a question about her status. "No I am a widow, a blessed widow, and I thank God! I wouldn't be a slave to God Himself, let alone a man."

Despite her low opinion of marriage, Helena's chumship with Olcott ripened into something approaching that institution. The two were soon sharing an apartment. Their flat, located in a pleasant brownstone building at the corner of

West 47th Street and Eighth Avenue, was quickly named, "The Lamasery" by their journalist friends. The place reflected Victoriana at its best—or worst—with bear skins, tiger skins, lacquer cabinets, placid Buddhas, palm trees, plush chairs and loveseats, a lion's head, stuffed lizards, a suit of armor, velvet swag draperies and cuckoo clocks. Amid the weird shadows, Helena cast a very special glow. The Lamasery was recalled by a *New York Herald* reporter as "one of the best known and most remarkable places of social resort in New York City." It was Helena who made the salon known and remarkable.

Was this enigmatic creature the agent of supernatural powers or merely a clever imposter? The great and near great of New York were divided but this merely added to the fascination of The Lamasery and its chatelaine. Reminiscing about the salon, a *New York Times* reporter recalled, "Talking by hours when the right listener was present, and speaking always 'as one having authority,' it is small wonder that Madame Blavatsky made her modest apartments a common meeting ground for as strange a group of original thinkers as New York ever held. Not all who visited agreed with her. Indeed, there were only a few who followed her teachings with implicit faith. Many of her friends who joined the Theosophical Society which she formed in 1875, were individuals who actually affirmed little and denied nothing. The marvels which were discussed and manifested in her rooms were to most of them merely food for thought. If the bell-tones of the invisible 'attendant sprite' were heard, as they were heard by scores of different persons, this phenomena was as likely to chaffed good naturedly by an obstinate sceptic as it was to be wondered at by a believer. Sensitive as Madame Blavatsky was to personal ridicule and to slander, she was truly liberal in matters of opinion, and allowed us as great latitude in the discussion of her beliefs as she took in discussing the beliefs of others."

Despite her unconventional living arrangement, Helena had become aggressively celibate and professed "a fierce scorn for anything remotely associated with the magnetism of sex." Believing herself to have been selected by higher beings to introduce ancient and forgotten wisdom for the spiritual renewal of mankind, a chaste image seemed mandatory. As interest in her slowly evolving philosophy grew, gossip began to circulate regarding Helena's improvident youth. Professing unconcern, she shrugged her shoulders airily. "Say what you will about my youth," she challenged. "From 1873 on, I am as pure as snow." How could she be held accountable for the past? That was clearly a different person, a restless, driven creature who had sought fulfillment in a variety of unconventional areas.

A statement was in order and she was ready with it: "As a public character, a woman who, instead of pursuing her womanly duties, sleeping with her husband, breeding children, wiping their noses, minding her kitchen, and consoling herself with matrimonial assistants on the sly behind her husband's back, I have chosen a path that led me to notoriety," she explained. "Even had I been all they accuse me of—had lovers and children by the bushel—who among that lot is pure enough to throw at me openly and publicly the first stone?"

Naturally there were many who tried but Theosophy flourished and survived the barrage. One hundred years later, the objectives of the international organization remain unchanged. Helena's tenets were and are: *to form the nucleus of a Universal Brotherhood of Humanity without distinction of race, creed, sex, caste, or color; the study of ancient and modern religions, philosophies, and sciences, and the demonstration of the importance of such study; and the investigation of the unexplained laws of nature and the physical powers latent in man.*

Like most religions, *Theosophy* (from the Greek, *The Wisom*) attempts to satisfy the universal craving to believe in the supernatural. Like Moses, Christ, Buddha and Mohammed before her, Helena claimed miracles and divine inspiration. The mysterious Protector who had guided her since childhood was introduced as *Master Morya,* a highly developed creature who had selected her as his earthly channel. Through Helena and the members of her slowly evolving Theosophical Society, the ancient esoteric traditions of occultism based on mystical insight and following Buddhist and Brahmanic theories would be made available to humanity at large.

Though Helena invariably attracted spirit manifestations

wherever she went and attributed them to her knowledge and manipulation of supernatural forces, she was wary of such phenomena and charged that mediums were taking fearsome risks with powers that they did not fully understand. It is only when one's spiritual nature is totally developed that the mortal can safely contact natural forces, she maintained. It is control over these forces that enables the mystic to bring about phenomena that is truly miraculous. Helena insisted that seance messages generally came from depraved spirits who merely stole the shapes of loved ones. These "shells" were condemned by their own sensuality to haunt the earth and frequently seduced weak-minded mediums into fraudulent practices.

In an effort to explain Theosophy to the world, Helena wrote—with some spiritual aid—the monumental volume, *Isis Unveiled*. Attacking both theology and science, she attempted to prove that the contributions of both were sterile because each had lost touch with the mainstream of all truth, the very ancient teachings of the occult that she had gleaned in her travels and was continuing to receive from Master Morya.

In his biography, *Old Diary Leaves*, Colonel Olcott describes how *Isis Unveiled* came to be. "In her whole life she had not done a tithe of such literary labor, yet I never knew even a managing daily journalist who could be compared with her for dogged endurance or tireless working capacity," he recalls. "From morning to night she would be at her desk, and it was seldom that either of us got to bed before 2 a.m. During the daytime I had my professional duties to attend to but always after an early dinner, we would settle down together to our big writing table and work for dear life until bodily fatigue would compel us to stop. She worked on no fixed plan but ideas came streaming through her mind like a perennial spring which is ever overflowing its brim. Higgledy-piggledy it came, in a ceaseless rivulet, each paragraph complete in itself and capable of being excised without harm to its predecessor or successor. Does this not prove that the work was not of her own conception; that she was but the channel through which this tide of fresh, vital essence was being poured into the stagnant pool of modern spiritual thought?"

Olcott assisted in this monumental task for two years, editing and correcting each page, for Helena sometimes found it difficult to express herself in English. Yet he insisted that "the book was hers alone, so far as the personalities on this plane of manifestation are concerned, and she must take all the praise and the all the blame that it deserves."

Years later he described nostalgically the "rare and never-to-be forgotten experience" of working with her. "We sat at opposite sides of one big table usually, and I could see her every moment. Her pen would be flying over the page, when she would suddenly stop, look out into space with the vacant eye of the clairvoyant seer, shorten her vision as though to look at something held invisibly in the air before her, and begin copying on her paper what she saw. The quotation finished, her eyes would resume their natural expression, and she would go on writing until again stopped by a similar interruption."

Helena continued to work in this fashion, sometimes not leaving The Lamasery for six months at a time. "It was not an uncommon thing for her to work seventeen hours out of twenty-four at her writing," Olcott said. "Her only exercise was to go to the dining-room or bathroom and back again to her table."

This was excitement enough for Helena. She wrote to her sister, Vera, of her involvement with the Egyptian goddess *Isis*, "I am solely occupied, not with writing Isis, but with Isis herself. I live in a kind of permanent enchantment, a life of visions and sights, with open eyes, and no chance whatever to deceive my senses. I sit and watch the fair good goddess constantly. And as she displays before me the secret meaning of her long-lost secrets, and the veil, becoming with every hour thinner and more transparent, gradually falls off before my eyes. I hold my breath and can hardly trust to my senses! . . . Night and day the images of the past are ever marshalled before my inner eyes. Slowly and gliding silently like images in an enchanted panorama, centuries after centuries appear before me. I certainly refuse point-blank to attribute it to my own knowledge or memory. I tell you seriously, I am helped and he who helps me is my Guru."

In this manner, *Isis Unveiled* grew to a manuscript of half-a-million words, too large for one volume. Consequently the book finally made its appearance in two very large volumes. It was sub-titled "A Master Key to the Mysteries of Ancient and Modern Science and Theology." The first book was called *Science;* the second, *Theology.* Colonel Olcott believed that he had been witness to a kind of miraculous double-header and was truly reverent.

The edition sold out within ten days though the press was anything but kind. Only the *New York Herald* was noncommittal. "It is one of the most remarkable productions of the century," their reviewer stated, probably too exhausted after 1,200 pages of esoteric doctrine to write more.

Now it was time to return to the source for even more enlightenment, Helena decided. The Masters who had guided her fate through so many turbulent years were calling her to India, she announced. Faithfully, Olcott prepared to accompany her.

Just prior to leaving, Helena became an American citizen on the very day that her five-year residency made her eligible. Learning that the first Russian woman in history was to be naturalized, the *New York Star* sent a reporter to cover the event. Asked to make the inevitable comparisons, Helena admitted that "American people are more polite to women."

"Are you in favor of female suffrage?" she was asked.

"I don't desire to vote myself, but I don't see why I shouldn't be allowed to," she answered. "All women should have the privilege. My papers say that I am a citizen, and are not *all* free and independent in this country? But I can't see how it makes much difference who votes and who doesn't." Helena felt her own concerns to be on the higher level of human liberation.

Arriving in India on February 16, 1879, she was her usual iconoclastic self—moving into the Hindu quarter, ignoring the all-powerful British overlords, disdaining to leave cards at Government House and tromping right and left upon cherished traditions. As could be expected, she was publicly disdainful of missionaries who were most un-Christian in their refusal to turn the other cheek. There were other foes as well. When Helena urged a revival of ancient Indian culture, the Criminal Investigation Department began a full investigation of her.

Malicious gossip swirled about Helena. She was a spy, she was a witch. She trafficked with the devil. More accurate, she was a determined woman who refused to conform to anyone's standards of what a high priestess should be. Freely admitting that she was a "rough old hippopotomus of a woman," Helena held court among her admirers in a dingy red wrapper, spotted and greasy, her fat fingers stained with nicotine. Her vocabulary liberally laced with four-letter words, she was an unlikely sibyl to speak out against the human weaknesses of sensual passion, ignorance, egotism, selfishness and fear of death. But that's exactly what she did. Despite Helena's scandalous past her thoughts were lofty and her courage equal to the task of expounding them.

In December 1880 the general council of the Theosophical Society met amid the feudal trappings of the maharajah's palace in Benares, India. In this setting of barbaric luxury, Helena reinforced the U.S. Constitution, insisting upon a universal pledge "to regard all men as equally brothers, irrespective of caste, color, race or creed." It was a slap in the face to the Hindu caste system as well as to British arrogance.

Helena's work was frequently aided at critical moments by a kind of astral telegraph system. The "Masters," Morya in particular, had a miraculous habit of showering Helena with written messages just when she seemed most in need of corroboration or support. To believers, this phenomena seemed no more surprising (or suspect) than the stone tablets of Moses. Non-believers tried with small success to prove these were her own invention. There were plots and counterplots but never conclusive evidence against her. Helena continued to reign imperviously. Her star was ascending. In less than a decade she had gone from a slum tenement to opulent Indian luxury.

At a large estate near Madras in Southern India, Helena held court in a magnficient mansion that had been purchased for her by devotees. Her magazine, *The Theosophist*, was an instant success and provided her with a handsome income and much personal publicity. Globetrotting intellectuals were drawn to this world-renowned personality and made her estate a mecca for the mystical.

Helena advocated a lifetime of strict discipline for those

seeking occult power. Disciples observed an ascetic regime of chastitiy, vegetarianism and meditation, while their Western guru appeared singularly lacking in self-control. It is arguable that she only adopted celibacy when she was too old and unattractive to do anything else. Even then she never forsook such sensual indulgences as meat and chain-smoking. "Follow not me nor my path, but the path I show," she advised and many thousands did just that.

It was an era too good to last. Helena came under fire from missionaries as an atheist, from scientists as a fraud and from the British government as a Russian spy. Driven at last from her spiritual paradise, the exhausted woman was literally hoisted aboard a Europe-bound steamer in a sling. It was a mortifying experience that seemed to have finally defeated her indomitable will. Struggling against her own temperament as much as from ill fortune, she cried out in anguish, "My heart is broken, I have no home, no one that I can rely on implicitly. I am tired of life. I am one too many on this earth."

A few months later when Helena's devoted friend, Countess Wachtmeister, arrived at Ostend, Belgium where Helena had taken up residence, she was shocked to find a doctor in attendance. Helena seemed totally exhausted, unable to remain out of bed for more than an hour at a time. The various remedies prescribed by the physician proved useless. In desperation the countess telegraphed England, pleading to Dr. Ashton Ellis that he come at once. The man, a Theosophist and an avid admirer of Helena's, left immediately and arrived at 3 a.m.

The two medical men, conferring together, diagnosed her illness as an acute condition caused by heart and kidney damage. Helena drew up a will disposing of her dwindling possessions. The countess was distraught for she had begun to detect "that peculiar faint odor of death which sometimes precedes dissolution."

The following morning as dawn was breaking, Countess Wachtmeister stole into the sickroom. To her surprise, she saw Helena watching her calmly. Rushing to the bedside, she gasped, "What has happened? You look so different?"

"Master has been here," Helena explained. "He gave me

the choice that I could die and be free if I would, or I might live and finish *The Secret Doctrine*. He told me how great my suffering would be and what a terrible time I would have before me in England—for I am to go there—but when I thought of those students to whom I shall be permitted to teach a few things and of the Theosophical Society in general, to which I have already given my heart's blood, I accepted the sacrifice. Fetch me some coffee and something to eat, and give me my tobacco box."

Her tremendous vitality miraculously restored, Helena plunged headlong into the writing of *The Secret Doctrine*. Soon settled in London, she disciplined herself to work a twelve hour day from six to six. The ultimate result was a manuscript three feet high containing more than 6,000 pages, truly an encyclopedic textbook on Theosophy. Once again, reactions were mixed.

Aside from the unwieldiness of the book's presentation, the worst that could be said by anyone was that Helena had borrowed from the wisdom of others. She merely laughed at the charge; it was something that she, herself, had maintained all along. During the course of writing the book, Helena had written to her friend, A. P. Sinnet, a noted newspaper editor and Theosopher, "*I live two lives again.* Master finds that it is too difficult for me to be looking consciously into the Astral Light for my *Secret Doctrine* and so, it is now about a fortnight, I am made to see all I have to as though in a dream. I see large and long rolls of paper on which things are written and I recollect them. Thus all the Patriarchs from Adam to Noah were given to me to see."

Besides the wisdom of the patriarchs, Helena also discoursed on Atlantis, communication between the South Sea Islands, the Druids, astronomy, astral man, the vedas, the origin of India, the third eye, Greek mythology, Lemuria and much more. It was a kind of everything you ever wanted to know about everything, as exhausting to the arms to hold as to the mind to contemplate.

Once again it was Helena the woman who came under attack when the book's philosophy defied the sceptical. She was described as "fat, gross, of abominable habit and intolerable tempers, swearing like a pirate and smoking like a chimney." It was all quite true, but what matter in the long run? Despite her personal lapses, Helena Blavatsky made magic creditable to a drab, materialistic world. The concept of reincarnation which she introduced to the West has been accepted by millions as a method where each individual soul will ultimately reap what it has sewn. Karma, the force behind this principle, is a doctrine of hope rather than pessimism.

When Helena wrote the passage, "One single thought about the past that thou has left behind will drag thee down and thou will have to start the climb anew; kill in thyself all memory of past experiences; Look not behind or thou art lost" perhaps she was thinking of her own wayward youth as well as why we are unaware of past incarnations.

Pitifully the aging woman attempted to make herself an eleventh hour virgin with a bogus medical certificate which also assured the doubting world that she had never had a "gynecological illness." A worse vehicle for sainthood never existed but in the end even that was unimportant.

Helena may have been a repugnant siren but she was a siren no less—capable to the very end of enthralling and infuriating, confusing and enlightening her bemused following. Before her death in London only a few months short of her sixtieth birthday, she had seen her ideas adopted throughout the world. The International Theosophical Center was established in India but a seed had taken hold in the West that would continue to flourish throughout Europe and the U.S. in decades to come.

Through the years the society has attracted such distinguished disciples as Thomas Edison; the Dutch artist, Piet Mondrian; the radical 19th century reformer, Dr. Annie Besant; General Abner Doubleday, the "inventor" of baseball; the Belgian playwright, Maurice Maeterlinck; the French astronomer, Nicholas Flammarion; and scientists, Alfred Russel Wallace and Sir William Crookes. At the death of Alfred, Lord Tennyson, poet laureate of England, a copy of Helena's mystical poem, *The Voice of Silence,* was found lying on a table beside his bed. Another admirer, William Butler Yeats, described her as "a sort of old Irish peasant woman with an air of humor and an audacious power," and told all who would listen that Madame Blavatsky had a bewitched cuckoo clock that hooted at will.

The saga of Helena's bizarre personality and magical gifts presents a fascinating if enigmatic aura; but it is the philosophy of this reckless, rebellious woman that matters. As a high priestess, Helena Blavatsky was much maligned. Her appearance was graceless, her manner eccentric. Some insisted that she was a fraud. Yet her esoteric views have new significance after more than a century.

Helena's final message, *My Books,* was written only ten days before her death on May 8, 1891—an event honored all over the world as White Lotus Day. In it she insisted once more that the ideas and teachings of her earlier works had merely been penned by her under spiritual dictation from Master Morya. In closing her essay, she quoted from Montaigne: "I have here made only a nosegay of culled flowers, and have brought nothing of my own but the string that ties them."

And then she added: "Is anyone of my helpers prepared to say I have not paid the full price for the string?"

5

Ernestine Shumann-Heink

A Valkyrie Come to Life

At fifteen, Ernestine Roessler—later known to the world as Madame Schumann-Heink—was rejected by the director of the Vienna Opera as being "too ugly to sing."

"Go home, quick," he advised, "and ask your kind friends who helped you to come to Vienna to buy you instead a sewing machine. Learn to be a dressmaker, maybe, or something like that—but a singer—an *opera* singer. Ach, no! Never—never in this world!"

Ernestine would prove him wrong. In a career that spanned sixty years, she became the greatest female singer of her time—a contralto the world will never forget. Born plain in a competitive society that demanded conventional prettiness, her talent and tenacity transcended surface charm. A woman snared again and again by her own anatomy, she refused to allow her destiny to be defined by traditional boundaries. Almost from infancy she established her sights and never wavered from her path. The obstacles seemed insurmountable, yet such was the power of Ernestine's courage and determination that she overcame them all.

"I am a soldier's daughter," she frequently said by way of introduction. Behind this vital statistic were pride and privation, discipline and denial; a birthright that contained the fighting spirit, sense of adventure and uncompromising fortitude of a true military hero. Born June 15, 1861, Ernestine was the first of many children of Hans Roessler, an Austrian Army officer who never rose above the rank of major, and his ailing wife, Charlotte.

Though an officer's pay was barely sufficient to sustain life, they educated their children in expensive private schools in hopes of preparing them for presentation to the royal family of Austria. Rigid standards of personal behavior were expected of them, however incompatible with the grim realities of daily living.

As the Roesslers shuttled about the Austro-Hungarian Empire from one garrison town to another, their lives were a continuing struggle for survival. Yet despite her trials, Ernestine's mother found time to teach the child operatic arias by ear. Then one day when the girl was nine, Mrs. Roessler was too ill for singing lessons. "I'm so hungry," the poor woman moaned. "How I should love a piece of Swiss cheese!"

"I will get it for you, Mama," the little girl promised.

"But my child, we have no money."

"I will get the cheese," Ernestine repeated. She ran all the way to the neighborhood grocery store. "Please, will you give me a piece of Swiss cheese?" she gasped breathlessly.

Warily, the grocery woman replied, "Where is your money?"

"My father will pay."

"Your father owes much money. Cheese you cannot have."

With tears in her eyes, Ernestine begged to pay for the cheese by singing. It was for her sick mother, she explained. "I will sing! I will dance! You may call your friends and neighbors to sit on the stairs and watch me," she pleaded.

The woman finally relented and there in a dismal grocery store in Graz, Austria, the plump, plain little girl who was destined to become one of the world's truly great singers made her first public appearance.

After the cheese incident, a retired opera star took an interest in Ernestine and agreed to instruct her. The child financed her lessons by stitching gloves after school for twenty-five cents a day, then purchased a battered piano on the installment plan and proceeded to give rudimentary lessons of her own. Ernestine patched the broken hammers of the piano with sealing wax and string, and rigged up a device so that she could push her baby sister's carriage back and forth while practicing.

Everyone who heard Ernestine sing responded to her unusually clear, bell-like tones. A group of admirers became so convinced of her ability that they urged her to audition before the director of the Vienna Opera and even agreed to finance the trip. Only Ernestine's father was disapproving. He considered an operatic career totally beneath the dignity of the daughter of an officer in the emperor's army. Only after many hours of pleading on Ernestine's part did he reluctantly give his consent.

But it was all for nothing. The opera director was unimpressed. "What's all the fuss?" he demanded sourly. "Look at her! Mein Gott! With such a face—and such poverty—nothing." He dismissed the fifteen-year-old Ernestine totally with an airy wave of his hand, shrugged his shoulders and turned away.

Returning home, heartbroken, Ernestine received little consolation from her father. "I thought so—I told you so!" he crowed delightedly. "That settles it. Now you go to school and learn to be a teacher. That at least is a *decent* profession, and I don't want to hear anything more, ever again, about theaters or actresses or opera singers—nothing like that! You be a teacher!"

Fortunately Mrs. Roessler was a woman with a mind of
her own. While pretending to agree with her husband, she
made it possible for Ernestine to secretly continue her lessons in his absence. When an invitation came to audition for
the Dresden Royal Opera, the girl was ready. This time a
kind friend loaned her ample money to make the trip with
the stipulation that some be spent for a new dress and particularly new shoes. (Ernestine was of necessity wearing old
army shoes!)

This time she wisely told her father nothing of the trip. "I
lied because it was necessary," she explained later. "Once
I'd heard a saying, 'A lie is too precious a thing to be
wasted!—which means, I suppose, not to throw away a
good lie on a poor occasion. So I made what I thought was a
very good lie for my necessity then—and I've never regretted it, either!"

Pretending that she was off to visit a schoolmate, the girl
journeyed alone to Dresden where her voice captivated the
opera director. A contract signed by the king himself was
hers along with a salary of $60 a month—twice that received
by her father.

To be a paid singer—and before long a featured singer—
seemed wonderful beyond belief to Ernestine. Then, three
years later, she impetuously ran off to marry Hans Heink, a
debt-ridden clerk, and this happy period came to a sudden
end. She was summarily discharged from the royal company
for marrying without the king's permission. "I was desperate at what I had done," she recalled in her memoirs fifty
years later. "The longing for my career was greater than
anything in my whole life. It *was* my whole life as I found out
too late."

"It was a big mistake, my marriage then. Let it go at that,"
she wrote matter of factly. "Heink didn't understand how I
felt, of course. No man ever can. So miseries piled up. We
didn't understand each other, like so many people who
marry."

From theater to theater Ernestine Heink went, begging for
a chance to sing. Hunger and unhappiness as Frau Heink did
little for her stage presence—nor did three successive preg-

nancies. Finally she found a stage. "You should be a comedienne," the director of the Hamburg Opera told the pale,
shabby girl. He hired her beautiful contralto voice for ten
dollars a month and gave her only light, comedy roles. "It
was the beginning of the terrible struggle for success, for my
career," she recalled. "I had only very small parts to sing and
a few hundred marks each year—and debts on top of it all.
During that time too, the first year a child and then every
year another. But I kept my courage somehow, I struggled
on."

Early in her fourth pregnancy, Hans Heink left his wife
with a mountain of debts which he had compiled. According
to German law, she was responsible for these and since there
was no money, all of her furniture was confiscated but one
bed and three chairs.

A small ray of hope pierced the gloom when Ernestine was
invited to participate in a benefit performance to take place in
Berlin. No fee was offered, not even expenses, but it was an
opportunity to show a large and influential audience what
she could do. "You must go," a neighbor urged. "I'll take
care of your children and lend you my rent money to buy a
train ticket." Such faith and generosity were inspiring from
the woman; she was the wife of a school teacher, had nine
children and was nearly as impoverished as Ernestine.

Traveling third class, Ernestine arrived in Berlin at 5 a.m.
The same kindly woman had provided her with sandwiches
for the journey but there wasn't a penny left for even a cup of
coffee. Ernestine sat for hours on a park bench waiting for
the theater to open. Later that day when her plight became
known to the opera company, she was given money to pay
for lodging. But before she had a chance to sleep her voice
had created a sensation.

Among those in the audience was Hans von Bulow, a
renowned director, who immediately engaged Ernestine to
sing at a festival at which the composer Johannes Brahms
was to be present. Her selection was a poem by Goethe
which Brahms had set to music and called *Rhapsody*. As
usual, Ernestine had nothing to wear but it made no difference. So great was her talent that the threadbare dress and
heavy walking shoes—she had no evening slippers—were

forgotten. At the close of the program Ernestine took numerous curtain calls flanked by the two great men— Brahms and von Bulow. It was a moment that she would cherish always.

When the thunderous applause began to fade, von Bulow turned with sudden interest to his new protege. "Why, this woman looks as if she was actually hungry—and she has little children, too! Well, I must do something about this," he promised. The conductor invited Ernestine to come to his family home twice a week for dinner. The generous leftovers were then taken home to her children. Nearly fifty years later she recalled the sauerkraut, smoked pork and dumplings with ecstasy.

Plans were made for her to take part in the forthcoming Mozart Cycle. She would sing all the big alto parts, von Bulow assured her. Unfortunately the idyl ended abruptly when the conductor discovered that Ernestine was pregnant. "Why," he ranted, "why must this baby come just at this time when we are giving the Mozart Cycle? Why couldn't it be born some other time just as well—why upset everything—spoil it all?" He refused to listen to Ernestine's protestations that she could perform in spite of her pregnancy. The sumptuous meals and Ernestine's dreams of performing·in the Mozart Cycle were ended. She went back to performing meager comedy roles for a miniscule salary.

Ernestine sang a few hours before the birth of her fourth child and then walked home, unable to afford a carriage. A friend delivered the baby for $2.50. A few days later she was back at the opera literally singing for her family's supper—a very sparse one. When not performing, Ernestine spent much of her time huddled in bed with the children for there was no money for coal. Life seemed unbearable and one day her reserve of courage melted away. On that cold November morning not long after the baby's birth, Ernestine gathered the children about her, dressed them in their thin, ragged clothing and set out for the railroad station. She had only one thought, to end this dreadful existence once and for all.

"I planned it all out," she explained. "I knew the time the train would pass and I would be ready." Ignoring the questions of the children, she pulled their stumbling bodies along with her. Like one possessed she plunged forward into the driving wind and snow. Close by the train whistle sounded. Ernestine held the children nearer to her, ready to leap forward into the face of the oncoming engine.

Suddenly little Lotta grasped her mother's hand. Looking up into Ernestine's agonized face, she cried out, "Mamma! Mamma! I love you, I love you! Take me home." Deeply ashamed, Ernestine turned back. She never again thought of killing herself. The old determination to succeed returned and would not again forsake her.

Now that same strong will that had driven little Ernestine Roessler to obtain the seemingly unreachable Swiss cheese carried her to the director of the Hamburg Opera. Storming into his office, she informed the startled man that she would be the first contralto of the opera company. "I shall be the first contralto of Germany! Of the world!" she shouted and then stalked out. The director chuckled, amused at her audacity. But a short time later when the company's prima donna turned temperamental, the man remembered her and invited her to sing the coveted role of *Carmen*. In those days singers were required to provide their own costumes. Ernestine, of course had nothing, but other members of the company came forth to offer her a choice of their garments. Some things were too large and others too small, but Ernestine was thrilled with them all—except for the shoes which were so tiny that she could barely walk from her dressing room to the stage. But walk she did, and sing too. She stepped onto the stage without a single rehearsal; her training with her mother, learning tunes by ear, served her well. The audience adored her.

Everyone was delighted except the company prima donna. Certain that Ernestine could never duplicate her success in other roles, she canceled out on two even more difficult parts, Fides in *Le Prophete*—one of the biggest contralto parts ever written—and Ortrud in *Lohengrin*. These, too, Ernestine mastered perfectly without a rehearsal. The director no longer laughed at Ernestine; he offered her a new contract and an opportunity to sing all the leads. She was to receive $200 a month—an immense sum to her at the time—and five dollars more for each additional performance after the first fifteen of the season. Eagerly she sang both dramatic and comedy leads, besides dancing in the ballet and reciting prologues. Everything asked of her she did—all the while perfecting her dancing and acting skills along with her singing. One month she sang thirty-two performances in succession. Hamburg was then known as the "factory" because so many new operas were being tried there. If they succeeded, they went on to become classics; if not, they were performed the one time and retired forever. The opportunity for variety and experimentation was limitless.

Ernestine acquired a reputation at this time that would last her entire career. At rehearsals she appeared torpid, almost dull, yet during the actual performance she was as exciting as forked lightning. She was an individualist who first had to work out each role in her own mind, determining the points that she would make and the manner in which she would make them. "I must do it my way. If I am not myself, I am no good," she said more than once. All agreed that she was far more than good. She was incomparable.

Her second marriage, this time to actor-tenor Paul Schumann, was far happier than her first but still presented many difficulties. Struggling to maintain both her career and her marriage, Ernestine once secretly arranged to have $3000 lopped off her own salary and added to that of her husband so that he would not be overwhelmed by her success. "To be a great singer means far more than just having a beautiful voice," she later admitted. "One must have brains, discretion, diplomacy and know-how to steer the boat when it is ready to go on the rocks, as very often happens in an operatic career—or in any other career that a woman undertakes."

When Ernestine received a long-sought invitation to sing in America her second child by Schumann was on the way. "Everything will be all right," she assured her horrified husband who was ill and jobless at the time. "What is another baby? We have so many," she said.

Maurice Grau, manager of the Metropolitan Opera Company was as angry at her pregnancy as von Bulow had been earlier. "Why didn't you tell me?" he demanded of Ernestine as they stood on the deck of the ship that had brought her to New York. "Nonsense," she shrugged. "What do you know about it? You know nothing about babies. I have had them many a time. I shall sing. You shall see. I shall make a grand success for you. This baby is nothing." Fortunately this time there was no choice; Grau had no one of Ernestine's magnitude with which to replace her.

The American debut of Madame Schumann-Heink took place on November 7, 1897. As the curtain went up the audience beheld the famous contralto in profile, her arms folded. It was the beginning of an electrifying performance that would evoke twenty curtain calls. One month later Ernestine's seventh child, George Washington Schumann, was born.

The boy's name—selected despite the official protest of the German Consul-General—reflected Ernestine's instant pleasure with America, its people and their lifestyle. She was delighted with the opportunity to break with the restrictions and formalities of the Old World. "I began to see freedom from many things," she wrote. "Then, too, I'm naturally a regular old tramp—just like my father in that way—a soldier. A soldier of fortune. That's what every artist is, if the truth be told. Yes, I liked change and adventure. It was in the blood, I suppose, for generations and generations. So from the beginning I loved the great and generous new country."

These were busy years. Schumann-Heink's initial debut in Chicago was followed by numerous appearances with the Metropolitan Opera Company in New York where her success was equally great. She sang before Presidents Roosevelt, Wilson and Taft at the White House and before the Kaiser and Kaiserin in Berlin. At a private concert presented at the request of Queen Victoria at Windsor Castle, Ernestine's rigid childhood grounding in protocol stood her in good stead. She was the only performer in the company to behave according to court etiquette. The queen, her son and daughter-in-law, the Prince and Princess of Wales, were charmed and the Duke of Connaught chose her to be his dinner companion. (The latter event was remembered by Ernestine more for the schnitzel and green peas than for the conversation.)

Ernestine's penchant for protocol never extended to her dress no matter how affluent she became. The famous soprano Melba once wrote of her friend's Paris debut, "Schumann-Heink had a face which was possibly more interesting for character than remarkable for beauty, and I am afraid that she did not at that time pay very much attention to her dress. I was interested to know what the French people would think about her. As soon as she came on stage, my heart sank! I bit my lips with pain at the fear of what the French would think, for it was an afternoon concert and Madame Schumann-Heink was in evening dress and presented an appearance which the Parisians evidently considered very odd. But then she began to sing and before she had finished her recitative in the Mozart aria, the whole house rose to its feet and cheered her! They had forgotten everything but her artistry."

The many triumphs of her French tour were marred somewhat when Ernestine returned to Germany where her children were living with Schumann's mother. Ferdinand, one of her youngest, toddled up to her and asked, "Is your name Mama? Is it?"

"If he had struck a knife into my heart, it would not have hurt so much as that," she said afterward. It was decided on the spot that the children would go to America with her. She would have one more baby, this one also literally nursed between arias. Though a warm, maternal woman who insisted upon mothering everyone, Ernestine never considered abandoning her career for the sake of her children. Art came first, other things and other people adjusted to the facts of her life.

Growing up as they did in opera the children saw their mother in many dazzling performances but none impressed them so much as her appearance as the witch in *Hansel and Gretel*. "Mother! Mother!" little Ferdinand screamed in horror when he beheld the performance for the first time and saw his mother, the witch, being thrust into the oven. A few minutes later when she appeared onstage apparently unharmed for her curtain calls, he cried out again. "There she is! There's Mother. They didn't burn her after all."

Madame Schumann-Heink became the most celebrated woman singer of the era—the darling of royalty and the star of the New York Metropolitan. But there were tragedies as well as triumphs. Her marriage to Schumann was marred by long separations necessitated by her demanding work schedule and his ill-health. They were thousands of miles apart when he finally died. Ernestine was performing a comedy role in Boston when she received a telegram stating that her gentle, kindly but often ineffectual husband had died. Backstage she closed her eyes and swayed on her feet an instant, but finished her part in the opera without missing a note.

In 1905 loneliness plus the total responsibility of eight children—one Schumann's by a previous marriage—may have prompted Ernestine's marriage to her secretary, William Rapp. Though Rapp had been faithful and efficient in his original role, the marriage didn't work and ended long before the actual divorce in 1914. However, the union served to make her an American citizen, something she never regretted despite the holocaust that followed in her native country.

She was performing in Germany when World War I erupted in 1914. "We were struck dumb," she recalled, when the news was announced during an intermission of *Parsifal*. "Then began the terrible excitement—the musicians rushed away. Most of them threw down their instruments and ran, without a word. The command had reached them to report immediately to their regiments. They were almost all soldiers, and many of them officers in the Austrian and German armies, and one and all had to go immediately to their posts. War had been declared between Austria and Russia. And God knows what was going to happen." Despite the dramatic exodus, Ernestine and a few remaining musicians and performers carried on and finished *Parsifal*. She had not only herself to think about but her large family traveling with her on this tour. It never occurred to her not to return to the United States. Her loyalties were entirely with her new country although much love and sympathy remained with the old. The problem now was how to get back. Told that only forty-eight hours remained in which to leave Germany before its borders were closed, she was frantic. Several members of her entourage were traveling without passports. No boats were leaving Germany, trains were stalled, credit frozen.

At last William Jennings Bryan, then Secretary of State,

heard of her plight and interceded in her behalf. Passports were granted and she was able to rent a car. This was merely the beginning of new terrors, for the roads were clogged with frantic refugees who tried to force their way into the car. "Somehow we got to Rotterdam and there waited for the boat to go," she recalled to her friends back home, in her Katzenjammer Kids English. "A boat that carried only 1,500 people they crowded 3,000 into it, so you can imagine how we were but we considered ourselves lucky enough to be on board and headed for America under any conditions."

One year later Ernestine's oldest son, August, announced that he would return to Germany to fight for the Kaiser. "I must fight for the Fatherland," he insisted, though she begged him to remain. "My duty is there and my duty is first, you have always told me. Now you want to keep me from that duty." Heartbroken, she said good-bye to him, knowing somehow that he would not return.

On April 7, 1917 the United States declared war on Germany. For Ernestine "this changed everything in the world. Although I had been an American citizen for some years, still I was Austrian born, and what I went through during the war is not easy to describe. I was in the deepest misery because of my boy, August, in Germany. Every telegram, every letter, everything was cut off," she explained.

It was then that she began to sing for the soldiers, crisscrossing the country visiting camps and hospitals. Her concert career was forgotten as she sang night after night. The thrilling voice brought tears to the eyes of lonely soldiers, her hovering, motherly manner and outrageous accent endeared her to all. She was "Mamma" Schumann-Heink to everyone. At one appearance she made in Denver, the audience numbered 14,000 while 25,000 more stood outside— incredible numbers for those days. At Camp Kearney, California, 100,000 thronged to hear her. All the while Ernestine's heart was torn by thoughts of dear ones suffering on both sides and fear for the safety of all her sons, for now the remaining boys had joined the American Army. George Washington was a stoker aboard a U.S. Naval transport which was torpedoed and sunk by a German submarine off the coast of Europe. Praying, he said later, "Please God, do not have it that my brother killed me," he made it safely ashore.

August was not so fortunate. He died aboard a German submarine on his mother's fifty-seventh birthday. Another son had died a few months before of an illness contracted in the army.

Even after the Armistice was signed, she continued to sing in hospitals throughout the country. Then thousands of Americans heard "Mamma" Schumann-Heink on her concert tours which were resumed as the country returned to normalcy. Millions still remember her radio performances of the witch in *Hansel and Gretel* each year at Christmas time. Her rendition of *Silent Night* at the conclusion of these programs left moist eyes all over the land.

So well known had she become that she was recognized on sight by fans in even the remotest areas of the country. In her memoirs she recalled her greeting by a tobacco-chewing resident of a tiny whistle-stop town where she had stopped briefly between trains. "Say, Ma'am, ain't you that big, fat famous female singer whose face we're seein' all the time in the newspapers?" he asked between squirts of tobacco juice.

"I'm a big, fat female, I'm sorry to say, and I am a singer," she admitted, "I'm sure of that—but about being so famous way out *here*—"

"Oh, yes," he interrupted, "yes, yer are! I know yer—know all about yor! You're the one we're always a readin' about. Why, we git our papers out here 'most every week—and thar was a picture in the last one looks jest like yer. You're her, all right!"

She was at this time five feet, three inches tall and weighed approximately two hundred pounds. She never dieted—perhaps recalling too well the days when she was hungry. Enrico Caruso often told of the evening he had encountered Ernestine in a New York restaurant. Before her on the table was a steak large enough to feed five.

"Are you going to eat that all alone," the great tenor asked.

"No," she replied, "mitt potatoes."

Despite her tremendous success, Ernestine retained an engaging humility—always remembering the hard times.

She often recalled herself as a young novice watching a great star consuming a huge bowl of macaroni. She had gone backstage to congratulate the diva on her performance, but words deserted her as she stared longingly at the luscious looking food. Will I ever be enough of a singer to afford macaroni like that whenever I want it, Ernestine had wondered. Years later, she was able to say, "Well, I've had my macaroni. Thank God, I can say it in my old age."

In 1933 Schumann-Heink astounded the critics by singing Wagner at the Metropolitan; though seventy-two years old, her voice was that of a young woman. Then capping her career at seventy-five, she appeared in her first movie, *Here's to Romance*. The reviews were sensational. "They say I am terrific, colossal, gigantic," she said, amused. "I don't think I like gigantic very much."

Ernestine had begun work on another film in which she was to co-star on November 17, 1936, when she was seized with a sudden throat hemorrhage and died the following day.

Dedication to her work had proved a tremendous source of strength. At the end of her days, she said, "My art is the one thing that has never hurt me, never disappointed me, never betrayed me. The long bitter years of sacrifice that one makes for a great career—to live always for one's art—that's the thing, the only thing that stays with one at the end."

6

Sarah Bernhardt

All Temperament and No Heart

Quand meme—withal and in spite of all. It was the motto of Sarah Bernhardt. One can almost see the shrug of Gallic shoulders as the great actress swept about the world gathering her rosebuds anywhere and everywhere. *Quand meme.* It personified the careless confidence of a woman who knew the true value of the moment *every* moment.

Fascinated by death all through her long life, Bernhardt was a consummate risk taker. The threat of earthly repercussions seemed slight as weighed against ultimate oblivion. "Life engenders life," she liked to say. "Energy creates energy. It is by spending oneself that one becomes rich."

Victorien Sardou, who wrote many of Sarah's greatest hits, said, "If there's anything more remarkable than watching Sarah act, it's watching her live." The man who was publicly Sarah's critic and privately her lover, Jules Lemaitre, wrote of her, "She could enter a convent, discover the North Pole, kill an emperor or marry a Negro king and it would not surprise me. She is not an individual but a complex of individuals." It is hardly surprising that such a woman would have reached the top of any profession that she undertook. Quite by accident, it was acting.

Sarah's penchant for risk taking may have been partially inherited from her mother, Julie Van Hard. Julie, a pretty Dutch milliner, had fled a middleclass existence to come to Paris with a young law student, Edouard Bernard. Though she was only twenty years old and spoke almost no French, Julie was anything but bereft when Edouard returned to Hol-

land shortly after Sarah's birth on October 23, 1844. In fact his departure seemed almost providential. Julie had discovered that mistressing had distinct advantages over millinery and that there were far more interesting prospects about than young Edouard. Of course a new baby was something of an inconvenience, but soon Madame Bernard (the "h" and "t" were added later) found the primrose path so profitably paved that she could afford to rent a suburban cottage for the infant Sarah and her nurse. It was an hour's carriage ride from Julie's place in Paris—a pleasant outing when she wished to impress some new man with her maternal concern and gentler instincts. These occasions, however, were rare. Thin, little Sarah had scant appeal; besides, there were soon two more daughters—Jeanne, and then Regina—to claim Julie's meager affections.

Practical as well as pretty, Julie became aware that the Parisian smart set was predominantly Catholic. So, in spite of her Jewish parentage, at age ten, Sarah was placed in a convent school. Catholicism immediately appealed to the girl's innate sense of the dramatic. The ritual, the pageantry, the incense were intoxicating to her emotion-starved soul.

Sarah flung herself into religion with a vigor that she would bring to all her fancies throughout life.

When she graduated at fifteen, she announced to a group of her mother's friends who had gathered to help decide her future: "I shall marry God." The idea of the daughter of the town's reigning courtesan becoming a nun was greeted with much hilarity, except for one dour man who suggested that "the silly fool be sent to a house of correction." Sarah sprang at this unfortunate person like a wounded animal, scratching his face and tearing at his hair. After the man had been rescued, another spoke. It was the Duc de Morny, the most prominent of Julie's lovers. With suave amusement, he had watched Sarah's display of emotion and offered some advice of his own. "The girl's a born actress," he announced with quiet authority. "She ought to be sent for training at the *Conservatoire.*"

Sarah was horrified by the suggestion. She recalled a once famous actress who had visited the convent. The woman was in the last stage of tuberculosis, obviously dying, a state the nuns attributed to her sinful career. "An actress?" Sarah gasped. "Never." She fled to her room but was eventually persuaded to attend the Comedie Francaise that evening. She, her mother, and the Duc de Morny occupied the dress circle box as guests of Alexandre Dumas—another of Julie's lovers. Years later, Sarah was to write of that night in her memoirs, "It was the curtain of my life rising."

The performance was Racine's *Britannicus*, a tragedy which reduced Sarah to sobs so noisy that people around them glared in annoyance. Julie went crimson with embarrassment; the Duc de Morny was amused but silent. It was Alexandre Dumas who placed a reassuring arm about Sarah's thin shoulders. Smiling, he acknowledged to Morny that he was quite right, the girl *was* destined for a stage career. Later that night Dumas walked the distraught Sarah to her room, bent his curly dark head over her hand and kissed it. "Goodnight, little star," he whispered prophetically.

What followed Sarah's decision to become an actress after all, was a classic case of not what you know but who you know. The Duc de Morny was half-brother of the Emperor

Louis-Napoleon, and one of the most powerful men in
France. How could the composer Auber, director of the Conservatoire, refuse Morny's protege? Sarah was to be allowed
to audition before the admissions committee, a jury made up
of the faculty and leading artists of the Comedie
Francaise—France's foremost theater. Sarah plunged into
her studies with "that vivid exaggeration with which I embrace any new enterprise," she later wrote. Dumas spent
hours coaching her on delivery and diction.

Although Auber was primed to like her, he alone could
not outweigh the five other jurors. The scrawny girl dressed
in black was not an appealing figure. The committee was
even less impressed by her choice of recitation, a Fontaine
fable. Its simplicity seemed almost an insult compared to the
ambitious offerings of the other contestants. Sarah's voice
broke as she began to speak. One of the panel members
snickered and the girl stiffened. Her stage fright gave way to
defiance—a trait destined to see her through many tight
places. *Quand meme.* She began again.

This time her voice was crystal clear. The tale of the prodigal pigeon was related with such fresh insight and tender-
ness that the judges were surreptitiously dabbing at their
eyes when the young aspirant stepped from the stage.

Sarah was accepted.

At home, Julie, who had not even bothered to attend the
audition, greeted the news with scant enthusiasm. As far as
she was concerned, her duties as a mother were fulfilled
when she found a wealthy young man who was not only
willing but eager to marry Sarah. The girl was clearly a fool
to reject such a splendid opportunity. She herself would not
give a sou for Sarah's chances as an actress. Who would pay
money to see a wraithlike girl with no style or beauty?

Sarah was determined to prove her wrong and practiced
hours on end, perfecting her diction and memorizing many
more parts than those assigned to her in class. Upon graduation, the good *duc* was again ready to prod destiny a bit
further. A word to the administrator-in-chief of the Comedie
Francaise brought an invitation for Sarah to become an apprentice.

In August 1862, when Sarah was not yet eighteen, she

made her debut in the role of *Iphigenie* by Jean Racine. The girl suffered from first-act stage fright and her classic Greek costume was most unflattering to a thin figure. At one point in the drama when Sarah stretched out her arms imploringly to Achilles, someone in the balcony cried out, "Watch out, Monsieur, or you'll impale yourself upon her toothpicks!"

Back in her dressing room between acts Sarah scrawled a defiant *"quand meme!"* across the mirror with grease paint. The characteristic last ditch defiance came to her rescue and her performance improved appreciably in the subsequent acts. The next day Francisque Sarcey, the most powerful critic in France—a man who attended a play every night of his life studying the skill of every actor or actress of note with meticulous concentration—wrote that Sarah "carries herself well and pronounces with perfect precision. That is all that can be said at the moment."

On January 15th of the following year she distinguished herself to the press in another fashion. During a historic ritual honoring the birthday of Moliere, Sarah was waiting backstage with the others who were to appear in a stately procession. Hopping excitedly about her was Regina, Sarah's nine-year-old half-sister who had wheedled permission to watch the pageant. Standing directly in front of them was Madame Nathalie, an actress described by a contemporary writer as "Nathalie the fat, the solemn, the old and wicked *societaire* (owner-member) of the Comedie Francaise."

When the time came to make her entrance this ponderous creature moved forward with regal tread, only to be yanked rudely backward. Regina had been standing—quite innocently—on Madame's train. Angrily the huge woman shoved the girl backward with such force that she fell against a stucco pillar and cut her head. Sarah came to her sister's defense with a violent slap on Madame Nathalie's fat jowly face. Stunned, the woman fell backward into a swoon knocking down a smaller actor in her path. The backstage commotion disrupted the entire Moliere ceremony.

The blow rocked more than Nathalie. It was a slap heard round Paris for it challenged the very foundation of the House of Moliere. Never since its founding in 1658, had an apprentice dared defy a *societaire*; actual physical violence was beyond imagination. While members of the Francaise were righteously indignant at such insolence, the press was titillated. Suddenly Sarah was the talk of the boulevards. At last an apathetic public had taken notice of the skinny nonenity who would one day be known as the Eighth Wonder of the World. It was only the beginning of coverage so vast that one historian stated that if all Sarah's newspaper and magazine reviews were pasted end to end, they would reach around the world and that a stack of her printed photographs would stand higher than the Eiffel Tower.

But all that was far in the future. In the meantime, there was an irate director to deal with. After summoning Sarah to his administrative office, Monsieur Thierry demanded that she make a public apology to Madame Nathalie. Sarah refused, counterdemanding that Nathalie make a public apology to Regina. Her resignation was requested and speedily received.

There followed a terrible period of enforced leisure. There was nothing for Sarah to do but bask in the reflected glory of a mother who merely tolerated her. Beautiful and coquettish Julie had come a long way in less than twenty years. Well kept by a series of influential men, desired by any number of others, hers was a glittering salon well attended by the Beautiful People of the day. Drawn like moths to a flame, they centered about the glamorous woman rarely noticing her intense sometimes sullen oldest daughter.

Once again Sarah's friend Alexandre Dumas came to the rescue. Thinking that her charms might be better appreciated away from the voluptuous Julie, he arranged for Sarah to visit friends in Brussels. While there she attended a masked ball and caught the eye of Prince Henri de Ligne, dressed as Hamlet. At the close of the final waltz, he is said to have given her a single perfect rose, the thorny stem wrapped in his own embroidered linen handkerchief.

The following day Sarah went riding in an open carriage. She was picture pretty in a wide-brimmed hat. Fastened to her padded bosom was the rose. Suddenly the dashing "Hamlet" of the night before came galloping down the Avenue Louise. Catching sight of Sarah, he rode directly to her side. Apparently it was one of those soul-to-soul moments of truth. The *quand meme* in Sarah rose to the fore as she impulsively returned with Henri to his palatial home on the Avenue de la Toison d'Or. (The rest of his family was fortuitously away for the month at a country estate.)

The biographer who first related this amorous episode was Sarah's granddaughter, Lysiane Bernhardt. The family chronicle was discreet but Lysiane did reprint a portion of a letter written to Dumas by his Belgian connection, a Mr. Bruce, who wrote in part:

> And so, my dear Dumas, your young friend Mlle. Sarah Bernhardt has conquered Brussels. At our ball she captured the heart of the Prince de L. . . I think they've been meeting. Do you resent my offering the girl too much to distract her from her troubles or do you congratulate me for giving an actress a means of freeing herself from prejudice?
>
> P.S. I have just returned from her hotel. Sarah has not shown up for eight days. It seems that she is traveling with "friends." I fear these "friends" merge into one person and they have not traveled farther than the Avenue de la Toison d'Or. That's what happens when you let a dragon-fly loose with a butterfly.

The idyl ended abruptly when Sarah received a telegram that Julie was seriously ill of a heart attack. Returning home, Sarah found her mother well on the road to recovery. But now it was she who did not feel too well. Sarah was pregnant.

She made the decision not to share the news with Henri. Since he had not pursued her to Paris, perhaps he did not wish to see her again, she reasoned unhappily. Scion of a lofty family, he was also handsome, charming and intelligent. Sarah was well aware that her lover was besieged by women of all kinds. The respectable ones would wish to share his title, the others would be delighted merely to help him spend his ample fortune. Her pride demanded that she stand apart. She would not allow any sense of obligation to spoil the happy memories that she hoped were mutual. Besides, Sarah candidly recalled, she had gone off with him so readily he might not even believe the child was his. Such a thought alone was enough to prevent the proud girl from revealing her story. Weeks passed and he did not contact her.

For months Sarah tried unsuccessfully to find acting jobs but was repeatedly turned down. At last her pregnancy became too far advanced to permit work even if she'd been able to get it. Ironically, despite the fact that Julie had born three illegitimate children of her own, she was "retired" now and refused to have her reputation sullied by a daughter's disgrace. Using the small dowry settled upon her by her father, Sarah moved into a tiny flat. Regina moved in with her. On December 22, 1864—attended only by a friend and neighbor, Madame Guerard, the twenty-year-old Sarah gave birth to a son whom she named Maurice.

Fortunately—for her funds were now totally depleted—Sarah was able to find a job as an understudy shortly after the boy's birth. Halfway through the run an actress fell ill and Sarah was given her part to play.

Once again her path crossed that of Henri de Ligne. The young prince came to Paris and saw Sarah's name on the theater bill. Obtaining her address from the stage manager, he went directly to her modest apartment. The existence of Maurice only seemed to add to Henri's resumptive ardor. He moved into the apartment and when he left Paris a few months later it was with the idea of obtaining parental permission to marry Sarah. One can imagine the reaction Henri's request had upon the aristocratic de Ligne family. An actress—an unknown actress, at that. An unwed mother—herself illegitimate. The whole thing was totally unacceptable. While Henri attempted to remonstrate with his parents, they secretly dispatched an uncle, General de Ligne, to buy Sarah off.

Though personally charmed by the young woman, de Ligne hued to the family line. Henri would be disinherited if he were to marry her, his position and fortune irretrievably lost. Tearfully Sarah agreed to send Henri away, but angrily disdained the offer of money.

When Henri returned, determined to marry her in spite of his family, Sarah nobly sent him packing. "Marriage would interfere with my career," she informed him. The moment was one of deep sorrow for her; she was truly in love with

Henri and her career at the time was anything but promising. It was a turning point in her life never to be forgotten. As the years passed the affair would gather added luster in her eyes.

The next day Sarah started a new job at the Odeon. Following General de Ligne's departure several days earlier, she had gone to the theater owner, Felix Duquesnel, and begged for a chance to prove herself. The Odeon, located on the Left Bank, was an innovative repertory theater very popular with the discriminating drama buffs of the day. Sarah knew an engagement there could provide the showcase to launch her once and for all.

The interview with Duquesnel was a historic one they would both recall. Years later he wrote of the memorable occasion:

> I beheld before me the most ideally charming creature one can dream of. Sarah at twenty-two baffles all description. She was not pretty, she was better than pretty. It was mid-June. She wore a China silk blouse of a delicate shade with beaded embroidery, her arms and shoulders thinly veiled, a feather fan at her belt and on her head a fine straw "skimmer" trimmed with tiny bells that tinkled at the slightest movement.

His partner, Charles-Marie de Chilly, was not so charmed. Chilly was familiar with Sarah's reputation for a fiery temper and saw no reason to take a chance on her. "If I were alone in this, I wouldn't give you a contract," he admitted frankly.

"If you were alone in this, Monsieur, I wouldn't sign it," was her equally candid retort.

But Sarah did sign. Her salary was 150 francs, just enough to maintain a menage that included Maurice, Regina and Madame Guerard—the faithful friend who now doubled as a maid and babysitter.

Sarah did poorly in her first production, better in the second and quite well in the third. After her fourth play the critic Sarcey, who had remained singularly unimpressed until then, wrote that she had "charmed her audience like a little Orpheus."

The big break came in *Kean,* a drama written by her old friend, Alexandre Dumas. Prior to the performance a dem-

onstration was staged by the largely liberal audience who
were piqued because the play was not one written by the
radical hero of the day, Victor Hugo, then in exile. As poor
Dumas entered, there were cries of "Down with Dumas!
Give us Hugo!" The clamor did not quiet as the first act
began and the speeches of the actors were inaudible.

When Bernhardt made her entrance as Anna Danby, the
crowd continued to shout and stamp. Once again the *quand
meme* spirit triumphed. Sarah walked to the footlights and
held out her hands in a gesture of appeal. Gradually the
audience quieted and she spoke with calm reason, reminding them of a forgotten sense of fair play. "Friends, you wish
to defend the cause of justice. Are you doing it by making
Monsieur Dumas responsible for the banishment of Monsieur Hugo?" The hecklers, apparently touched by the
young woman's courage, recognized the foolishness of their
own actions. Their good nature restored, they settled back to
enjoy the performance. There was much to enjoy. From then
on the only demonstration was enthusiastic applause for the
excellent job that Bernhardt did in her difficult part. At the
end the audience demanded a solo curtain call—her first. It
was a heady moment, never to be forgotten.

Even de Chilly was delighted. "You were good," he admitted, "wonderfully good!" Sarah was unimpressed by his
sudden capitulation. "You find that I've grown plumper,
Monsieur?" she twitted him. (Only a few weeks before he'd
called her "a needle automated by four pins.")

Duquesnel and de Chilly informed Bernhardt that her salary would be increased to 250 francs a month. But even more
gratifying, that night for the first time a crowd of admirers
gathered about the stage door to cheer and toss flowers as
she left the theater. "Back in my room that night," she wrote
years later, "I felt so rich . . . so rich I was afraid of robbers."

Sarah Bernhardt's popularity increased steadily. The
nights when her name appeared on the bill were invariably
sold out. Members of the Odeon rotated in many roles and
there were at least fifty new productions each year. Bernhardt thrived on the energetic, hard-working atmosphere;
the next six years were among the happiest of her life. Later
she wrote nostalgically of this period:

> Ah, the Odeon! The theater I loved most of all. I was very
> sorry to leave it. We were all fond of one another and
> everyone was happy. Duquesnel was a manager full of wit,
> gallantry and youth. I remember the few months that I had
> spent at the Comedie Francaise. Nothing but affected gos-
> sipy, jealous people . . . but the Odeon was ideal. The only
> thought was to put on plays. We rehearsed morning, after-
> noon, all the time. I adored that. I worked hard and was
> always ready to take anyone's place, as I knew every part.

Among Sarah's roles were leads in two plays by George
Sand, *Francoise de Champi* and *Le Marquis de Villemer*. The
famous writer who was then in her sixties was delighted by
the younger woman's talent and enthusiasm. The two took
long walks together in the Luxembourg Gardens. During
one of these strolls Sarah confided, "Oh, Madame Sand, I
would sooner die than not be the greatest actress in the
world!"

In keeping with this determination was Bernhardt's total
dedication to perfection. She was whole-hearted, single-
minded, conscientious and indefatiqueable. Nothing, where
acting was concerned, was ever too much effort for her. She
was never content to say "That will do," much less, "That
will have to do." Once while preparing to play the part of
Cleopatra, a friend saw Sarah painting her palms a terra
cotta red. "Why?" she was asked. "No one in the audience
could possibly see it." "I shall see it," the actress explained.
"If I catch sight of my hand it will be the hand of Cleopatra."

Sarah's personal style developed during her Odeon days
along with her professional talent. She moved to a larger
more luxurious flat and engaged a cook and a maid. The first
of her much talked about menagerie was acquired at this
time: two dogs, and a pair of turtles who had the run and the
crawl of the apartment. Among her human satellites were
Gustave Flaubert and Prince Napoleon. It was a giddy,
glorious time which only war itself could disrupt.

As the turbulent tide of the Franco-Prussian War boiled
over France, many fled fearing that Paris might be attacked.
Sarah saw to it that her son Maurice, her sister Regina and
their nurse were among them. Hopeful that the Prussian
invaders would soon be halted, she insisted upon remaining

behind and maintaining a business-as-usual stance. But as conditions at the front worsened, the time came when there was neither heat nor gas for illumination and the Odeon was shut down.

Eager to do something to help the thousands of wounded soldiers that were being brought into Paris each day, Sarah appealed to Count de Keratry, a former lover who was now Prefect of Police:

> I hope that in remembrance of the little girl you once knew, you will listen to the young woman who, having known suffering now wants to ease, as much as possible, the sufferings of others. I request in my name and in those of my companions a permit to install an emergency hospital in our foyer and lobbies.

Count de Keratry was touched by Sarah's eloquence—and possibly by memories of their passion—he gave her not only the permit, but food, medical supplies and finally his own fur-lined overcoat. The coat Sarah passed on to a mobile guard whose hand had been shot off—the poor man had been forced to give up his bed to the more seriously wounded and was convalescing on the cold floor. Word got around and soon Sarah's few friends who had remained in the now besieged city were advising one another, "Don't go near the Odeon in any warm clothes. Sarah Bernhardt will rip them off your back for her invalids." It was not an exaggeration. Keratry raided the Empress Eugenie's larders in the Tuileries and subsequently presented Sarah's makeshift hospital with one hundred bags of coffee, ten barrels of wine, forty cases of biscuits and one thousand jars of preserves. Additional donations resulting from Sarah's persistence and charm were two barrels of brandy from the Baron Rothschild, five hundred pounds of chocolate from the grocery magnate Felix Potin, and enough Dutch linen from that country's ambassador for thousands of bandages and three hundred nightshirts.

Sarah's field hospital was considered the best equipped in Paris. But this was in the early days of the siege; Paris had not yet begun to starve.

Bernhardt, long a creature of fragile health who fainted at

the sight of blood, took over complete management of the hospital and was its head nurse as well. Assisting her was her cook who installed a stove in the first tier of boxes and worked non-stop making soup and tea. Helping with the nursing was another actress and Sarah's lifelong friend, Madame Guerade. The three women literally worked day and night, catching only a few hours of sleep in weeks. Advising them was a Dr. Duchesne, who had deserted his society practice to work at the hospital.

The severest winter on record settled upon them. Sarah—who abhorred any outdoor activity and who had kept a crackling fire in her dressing room nearly the year round—spent entire nights on the battlefield administering brandy to the wounded who were dying of cold. Back at the hospital, she held the basin while Dr. Duchesne amputated mutilated legs or probed into raw flesh for shrapnel. The same delicate Sarah who was offended by smoking now coolly but compassionately dressed wounds that reeked of gangrene.

As ice formed over the Seine, the city's supply of coal ran out completely. Sarah and her workers tore out theater seats to burn, then ransacked the cellar for old scenery and thrones to be thrown one by one into the furnace. As food grew more and more impossible to obtain, zoo animals, cab horses and household pets were killed. At the butcher shop a rat sold for two francs, a sparrow for one and a quarter. Often the actress and her hospital staff went without food themselves so that their patients might have some.

Among the soldiers cared for at the hospital was a young military school student recovering from a shrapnel wound in the shoulder who was so enamored of Bernhardt that he considered his pain a small price to pay to be under the same roof with her. When he finally recovered he made a reluctant departure but not without a blushing request that his idol autograph one of her publicity pictures. (Years later when Sarah at age seventy-four was once again giving tirelessly of herself to aid the soldiers of France, they were to meet again. The adoring boy was now a man, Marshal Ferdinand Foch, commander-in-chief of the Allied Armies of World War I.)

In January 1871, during the sixteenth week of the siege,

the Prussians began the indiscriminate bombing of Paris. Hospital flags merely supplied fresh targets to the merciless enemy. Sarah moved her charges to the safety of the basement, which was rampant with rats and filled with sewage that had escaped from broken water pipes. Finally after the nineteenth week of siege, Paris capitulated.

Shortly thereafter the revolutionary Commune erupted and the government fled to Versailles. Once again Sarah refused to leave, but this time was forced to change her decision. The new Prefect of Police, Roul Rigault, had a personal grudge against her which stemmed from a time when Sarah had rejected a play that he had written with the words, "Monseiur, your play is unworthy to touch, let alone to read." The man's harassment became so menacing that Sarah was finally forced to flee to Saint-Germain-en-Laye where she sat out the political holocaust with her family. After slaughtering more than twenty thousand people the Communards were finally ousted in May.

As a semblance of normalcy returned to Paris, Sarah moved back with her family. The Odeon was repaired and refurbished; Sarah appeared in the first of many hits. At twenty-six, she became the unquestioned goddess of the Left Bank.

Bernhardt had learned to live life very fully. Throughout her sickly childhood she knew that no one expected her to live into her twenties and the consumptive girl had developed a morbid fascination for death. Almost as though to test out her fears, she ordered a rosewood coffin and posed in it during the early Odeon days. At home, her eclectic furnishings included a skull and a skeleton. She visited executions and dissecting rooms and once feigned death so effectively backstage that Duquesnel announced her demise to the audience and summoned a hearse. In this bizarre manner she lived with the death she believed imminent. But Sarah was paradoxically drawn to life.

She took balloon rides, kept wild animals for pets, ran up extravagant bills, painted and sculpted so well that her work was frequently exhibited. She also enjoyed enumerable love affairs. "Life is short, even for those who live a long time," she wrote. "We must live for the few who know and appreciate us, who judge and absolve us, and for whom we have the same affection and indulgence . . . We ought to hate very rarely, as it is too fatiguing; remain indifferent a great deal, forgive often and never forget."

In the spring of 1873 Bernhardt received a hand-delivered envelope bearing the engraved crest of the Comedie Francaise. The first theater of France was asking her to return. The terms were inviting, particularly the excellent salary of 12,000 francs—2,000 more than she was then receiving at the Odeon. But even more appealing was the opportunity to return in triumph to the theater from which she had parted an unlamented nobody nine years earlier. Furthermore it was an opportunity to create a lasting name for herself by competing with the great actors of her day in the leading theatrical company in the world.

Yet the choice was not so easy. At the Odeon she was loved and admired by her colleagues, at peace with herself, and yet challenged and stimulated by her surroundings. She debated the decision and then finally said a sad farewell to the Odeon. Sarah demanded much more from life than mere peace of mind. Here at last was a stepping stone to the world.

Sarah's return to the Comedie Francaise caused a furor in the theater world, largely brought about by the writings of the critic Francisque Sarcey who was totally captivated by Bernhardt's skill. Still another critic, Theodore de Vanville, wrote of her re-admission:

> Make no mistake; the engagement of Mlle. Sarah Bernhardt at the Comedie Francaise is a serious revolutionary fact. Poetry has entered into the house of dramatic art; or, in other words, the wolf is in the sheep-fold.

Not surprisingly, this did nothing to endear Sarah to the apprentices at the Comedie who were already incensed at the return of the former *infant terrible* now proclaimed a star. Sarah was dismayed not only by their hostility but by the Establishment solemnity and conservatism. She missed the gaiety and enthusiasm of the Left Bank and the Odeon, yet realized those days were gone forever.

By now Sarah Bernhardt was the most talked about

woman in Paris with much of the interest centering about
her amours. One of the most satisfactory of many liaisons
was with Jean Mounet-Sully, considered to be the hand-
somest actor in France as well as the greatest tragedian. They
had been slightly acquainted while both were engaged at the
Odeon, but the casual friendship deepened into much more
when Mounet-Sully joined the Comedie Francaise. Sarah
was reported to have been totally stunned when she encountered him there for the first time.

"It's not possible, Mounet!" she gasped. "What's happened to you?"

"What do you mean?"

"But you're very handsome!"

"So I've been told."

"But you weren't like this at the Odeon."

"I believe I was."

"Come on now. I'd have noticed it."

"Perhaps you didn't have time to notice me."

Soon all of Paris was busy noticing the two of them notice
each other. Appearing opposite one another for the first time
in Racine's *Andromache*, Sarah and Sully were launched as
France's greatest acting team. The pair kept busy offstage as
well for several years, remaining lifelong friends when the
affair ended.

The romantic duo's greatest onstage triumph was *Phedre*.
Writing of Sarah in the title role, the critic Jules Lemaitre—
who would later be a lover too—wrote that she put into her
role "not only her soul, her spirit and her physical charm,
but her sex. Such bold acting would be shocking in anyone
else; but nature had deprived her of so much flesh and having given her the looks of a chimeric princess, her light and
spiritual grace changes her most audacious movements into
exquisiteness." In his own critique, Sarcey wrote: "This is
nature itself served by a marvelous intelligence, by a soul of
fire, by the most melodious voice that ever enchanted
human ears. This woman plays with her heart, with her
entrails."

By now she had moved from her apartment and had
plunged into debt to buy a small but elegant home designed
by the fashionable architect Felix Escalier. She now kept a

staff of eight servants and owned two carriages. The menagerie had grown to include lions, a parrot and three monkeys.

Bernhardt entertained lavishly and often. Among the guests were Emile Zola, Victor Hugo, Alexandre Dumas (the son of her girlhood confidant), Louis Pasteur, the poet-playwright d'Annunzio and Oscar Wilde—all close friends. A not infrequent guest was the Prince of Wales, later Edward VII, rumored to be still another lover.

Gamaliel Bradford, a contemporary and biographer of Sarah, observing the amorous parade felt that Sarah never really gave herself or lost herself in any of them. "There was infinite curiosity, eagerness, the sense of adventure, the desire to probe, to investigate, to explore, other thoughts, other hearts, other souls," he speculated, "but there is no suggestion of complete abandon or self-forgetfulness. Perhaps to the very end Sarah retained something of the cynical childish impression that she imbibed from her mother's very promiscuous establishment: 'My mother's house was always full of men, and the more I saw of them, the less I liked them.'"

Yet all her life Sarah did enjoy the company of men and could rarely resist a charming one. She was attracted by talent and her influence was invariably beneficial. No one ever accused Sarah of "selling herself," but she did enjoy exacting a tribute of sorts. To painters she might say, "If you love me, then paint a masterpiece and dedicate it to me." To poets she might insist, "If it is true that you love me, you will write a poem about me that will live when we both are dead." The younger Dumas said of Sarah, "She drives me mad when I am with her. She is all temperament and no heart; but when she is gone, how I work! How I *can* work!"

As the years passed at the Comedie Francaise and Sarah continued to bring extra revenue into the communal coffer, the closeknit group came to accept and finally even to like her. Eventually the persistent echo of Sarah's slap died away and even Madame Nathalie saw decided compensations in Sarah's box office appeal. Upon retirement from the company each member was entitled to a benefit performance given in his or her honor. The proceeds were then given to the retiree as a farewell tribute. Those participating in the program volunteered their talents as a goodwill gesture. When the day came for Madame Nathalie's departure, she was quick to solicit Sarah's services. Never one to hold a grudge, Bernhardt gave generously of her talents. Surely she could afford to be generous, the whole world was waiting. Having conquered the Comedie Francaise, she was beginning to cast about for bigger things.

First came London. Despite the fact that she spoke no English, Bernhardt was a sensation. Ellen Terry, England's most popular actress, wrote of Sarah in her own memoirs: "She was as transparent as an azalea only more so; like a cloud only not so thick; smoke from a burning paper describes her more nearly." The two became close friends, referring to one another as "Sallie B." and "Nell." Once when a mutual acquaintance, the actor Henry Irving, spoke of growing old, Sarah leaned across him to Ellen and said, "My darling Nell, there are two people who shall never grow old . . . you and I." In a sense, they never did.

Bernhardt's enthusiasm for the theater was undiminished, but some of the ensuing social whirl had become a bore. She rarely wrote a note of thanks for the many courtesies she received and when she did it was invariably an indecipherable scrawl. "I am too busy living to finish my words," she explained.

Following her London triumph, Sarah began to seriously consider breaking with the Comedie Francaise. Though well aware of the prestige connected with France's top national theater, she still chafed at the restraints placed upon her by being merely one of an acting commune. The ponderous institution was often impeded by tradition and long established rules—rules that Sarah had begun to think might be meant to be broken—at least by herself.

The break finally came when Sarah was forced to play a part that she detested; the role of Dona Clorinde in *L'Adventuriere* was not only moralistic but dull. A contemporary critic said of Sarah in this connection: "From the very beginning to the very end of her career nobody was ever more absolutely certain of what she could do and what she could not do, and whether or not she could make something or nothing of a part; and those who persuaded her to act against her instinct in these matters invariably lived to regret it."

Such was the case with *L'Adventuriere*. Struggling half-heartedly with the part, Sarah frequently forgot her lines. One day when the playwright himself remonstrated with her, Sarah retorted, "What do you want me to do? I know I'm bad, but not as bad as your lines!" The day before the play was to open, Sarah developed a bad sore throat and laryngitis. Too exhausted to go for fittings, she begged the director to postpone the opening for another week— something quite easily arranged in a repertory theater. He refused.

The opening was a disaster. Sarah's gown was miles too big, her voice that of a foghorn. She was frankly awful and well aware of it. After reading every one of the blistering reviews, she sat down and wrote the following letter:

> Monsieur L'Administrateur. You forced me to play when I was not ready . . what I foresaw came to pass. The result of the performance exceeded my expectations . . . This is my first failure at the Comedie and it shall be my last. I warned you on the day of the dress rehearsal and you ignored my warning. I keep my word. When you receive this letter I shall have left Paris. Be so kind, Monsieur l'Administrateur, as to accept my immediate resignation.

By resigning Sarah forfeited 40,000 francs of retirement money set aside for her, as well as setting in motion a 100,000 franc breach of contract suit which dragged on for twenty years. It seemed of small concern at the moment. "I'm free to do as I please, anywhere I please," she thought. *Quand meme.*

Paris as well as the Comedie was thrown into an uproar. Sarah was denounced as a deserter, which she later denied. Likening the Comedie Francaise to the ensign of her country's art, she admitted that she had refused to serve in the ranks. "But does that make me a deserter?" she asked. Sarah insisted, instead, that her job was to unfurl the flag to the winds of other nations, to make it known beyond the frontiers.

That flag was soon to be unfurled in America where Sarah was both a critical and a financial success. Here the most popular play was a new production, *La Dame aux Camelias,* which everyone insisted upon calling *Camille*. Not surprisingly, Sarah found it easy to portray the ailing young coquette who sends her adored lover away to oblige his titled family—she had played the part in real life nearly twenty years before!

If this titillating play with its view of depraved Paris wasn't enough to send Americans streaming to the box offices, the clergy of the country seemed to be united in the effort to make Sarah a millionaire. By denouncing this "whore of Babylon" from their pulpits they ensured her an avid audience. The Episcopal Bishop of Chicago did the job so effectively that Sarah's agent sent him a thank you note:

> Your Excellency,
> I am accustomed, when I bring an attraction to your town, to spend $400 on advertising. As you have done half the advertising for me, I herewith enclose $200 for your parish.

Traveling aboard her own train, the "Sarah Bernhardt Special"—containing three Pullmans, plus her own "Palace Car"—she followed a crushing schedule but seemed to thrive on it. Sarah was constantly busy reading new plays, trying them out with members of her cast, and rehearsing the standards. This was to be Sarah's touring routine, strictly adhered to for the next forty years of her life.

Quoting an American manager, her biographer Cornelia Otis Skinner noted of Sarah, "Her energy and enthusiasm are endless. I never saw her show the slightest fatigue; I never saw her bored, I never saw her miss a beautiful bit of scenery from the car window or fail to appreciate a good joke."

During this first tour, Sarah added two black snakes and an alligator to her menagerie. The alligator followed her about the train and even under the covers of her bed. One wonders what Angelo, Sarah's leading man and resident lover, thought of this.

When Sarah returned to New York from her cross country tour, she had given a hundred and fifty-seven performances in fifty-one cities. As she prepared to leave for Paris, the magazine *Judge* reported thusly:

> We shall miss the tearing terror of Sarah Bernhardt. We shall

miss her smile of love and her expression of trust and confidence. We shall regret the absence of that thin countenance on whose surface appeared more of the counterfeited soul than anybody has succeeded in picturing. We shall miss that magnificently cultured voice, those secluded eyes, those conspicuous teeth, that serpentine twist of the body and the tiger too. But our loss will be her gain. She takes about half a million in clear profits with her . . .

The actual figure was $194,000.

For some reason Sarah's triumph in the United States seems to have piqued Paris. It seems her fans considered it an insult to France that she would have performed the plays of Racine and Moliere before illiterate Americans, too vulgar to appreciate them. No cheering crowd was waiting at Gare Saint Lazare to greet her arrival. No manager came forward with an offer, no playwright proffered a new script.

Prior to Sarah's departure, Victorien Sardou had promised to write a play especially for her. Declaring that he could hardly wait to begin, Sardou had promised to have the script ready when she returned. Raymond Deslandes, manager of the fashionable Vaudeville theatre, had been eager to commence production of any vehicle written by Sardou and starring Bernhardt. Now both were conspicuous in their absence. "Don't call us, we'll call you," was the essence of their answer when she attempted to contact them. All of Paris appeared to have turned its back on the returning adventuress.

More than hurt pride was involved in Sarah's rebuff. The profits from the American tour—large as they were—could not last long at her present rate of spending. She was a woman who adored shopping—gowns, jewels, paintings, furnishings, pets. Her lifestyle was one of largess in every sense. It suited her well and she had no intention of cutting back. Further, even if Sarah had been willing to curb her own impulses, there was her son, Maurice. Maurice had grown to near manhood adoring his glamorous, affectionate, open-handed mother. She was not about to alter the give and take of their relationship to the slightest degree. It pleased Sarah to indulge Maurice every bit as much as it pleased him to accept her bounty. She would find a solution to the problem.

As Bastille Day approached, Sarah hit upon an idea. It was to be one of the supreme *quand même* moves of her life. A lavish celebration had been planned to commemorate the patriotic holiday with all the heads of state in attendance. An opera was to be presented, Mounet-Sully would read a patriotic poem and—as the grand finale—Marie Leonide Agar was to recite the *Marseillaise* accompanied by a full orchestra.

Agar had remained a friend of Sarah's since Odeon days, as had Agar's maid, Hortense (who invariably referred to Sarah as "La Divine.") Sarah arranged a secret interview with the maid and persuaded her to play a trick upon her mistress. Hortense was to present Agar with a message that a young officer—a current lover—had been injured in a riding accident and had been rushed to a hospital in Tours. Upon hearing the news Agar departed immediately for the train station, first instructing Hortense to go directly to the gala directors and inform them of her inability to appear so that they might arrange a replacement. Hortense neglected to perform this duty.

The gala progressed successfully. The audience greeted the opera warmly. Mounet-Sully finished his poem to enthusiastic applause. Then just as he swept offstage, Sarah appeared in the wings. The two managers who were in charge of the event stood transfixed as though viewing an apparition. They were aware of Sarah's current unpopularity with the people and were certain that the gala had been ruined. "Don't worry," she reassured them. "I have far more to lose than you."

Sully watched as his former mistress dropped her cloak backstage and stood before them, a delicate column of pristine white. Her only adornment was a tricolor streamer crossing from one slim shoulder to her tiny waist. The drums started to roll and the president rose in his box followed by the entire audience who now stood at attention. There was a collective gasp of astonishment as Sarah walked out onto the stage. The music began and Sarah's voice could be heard reciting the thrilling anthem with fresh poignancy.

At the close when she unfurled and held aloft the flag of France, the audience went wild, shrieking, cheering, shouting, "Sarah! Our Sarah!" President Grevy tossed a large bouquet of roses at her feet. The audience simply refused to part with Sarah until she recited the whole thing over twice, each time receiving the same thunderous ovation.

All of Paris was delirious with excitement over Sarah's triumph, her great talent rediscovered through sheer audacity. Even Agar was delighted and laughed good naturedly over the hoax played upon her. She had enjoyed a pleasant and unexpected night with her lover made all the more rapturous by finding him strong and unhurt. How could she be angry with her old friend?

Once again Victorien Sardou was making overtures to Sarah. Already he had a splendid manuscript, a fantastic play called *Fedora*, tailored perfectly to Sarah's gifts. (It was to be the first of a series that would make them the most successful author-player team in theatrical history. "There is but one Sarah and Sardou is her prophet" would become a pleasant joke known to everyone in their day—but that was in the future. In the meantime Sarah was to have her revenge.)

The following day when Sardou and Raymond Deslandes appeared at Sarah's door, she greeted them sweetly and listened politely as they babbled on about her salary which would be 1000 francs a performance with a guarantee of one hundred performances—a most generous sum in those days. Sarah then gently but firmly insisted that she could not possibly appear for less than 1500 francs a performance plus twenty-five per cent of the net profit. Deslandes very nearly suffered apoplexy but eventually yielded. "How soon can you begin rehearsing?" he gasped at last.

Sarah paused, smiled, then leveled them with the news: "Not for six months, Monsieurs. I've signed for an extensive tour of Europe." Sarah was certain that she could carry off her strategy and win. The tour would be a financial coup and the people of Paris would be waiting eagerly for her return. She was correct on both counts.

In that glittering era of royalty Bernhardt was the toast of the Romanoffs, the Bourbons, the Hapsburgs. But the poor adored her as well. In London, an old woman set up a shrine in a corner of her shabby lodgings. On it were placed a number of objects that Sarah had touched: gloves, a handkerchief, a hairpin. At a tiny railroad station while traveling in Scandinavia Bernhardt was awakened in the night; more than a hundred peasants were standing on the tracks waiting for her train to pass through and would not move until they had seen her.

Only in Odessa, Russia, was this apparent adoration missing. There anti-Semitism was so rampant that Sarah would have been stoned to death if the police had not rescued her. But the reception in St. Petersburg was entirely different—a luxurious red carpet was unrolled across the snow for Sarah to tread upon. A reception honoring the actress was held at the Winter Palace where Alexander III, czar of all Russians, bowed to *her*.

Russia was memorable for yet another reason. It was here that Sarah met and fell in love with Jacques Damala. Arrogant and vain, eleven years her junior, Damala was known as the "Diplomatic Apollo" because of his amorous exploits while serving in the Greek diplomatic corps. Always before this Sarah had retained an element of detachment throughout her numerous affairs; though she referred to herself as a *grand amoureus*, her liaisons had always existed in the background of her life. They had been romantic, pleasurable—often solidified by a mutual absorption in the theater—but contained more camaraderie than all enveloping passion. Each had followed a prescribed course invariably ending in amiable friendship. Now at thirty-seven, Sarah was a victim of that grand passion she had portrayed so many times upon the stage.

Accustomed to awe and diffidence from men, she was stunned and then challenged by Damala's seeming indifference. His casual unconcern only served to fire her own ardor, now grown to a delicious insanity. Soon the Bernhardt-Damala affair was the talk of St. Petersburg, for Sarah would go nowhere without him. Philippe Garnier, the actor who had been occupying the usual leading-man-resident-lover spot, conveniently left the company. Damala resigned from the Greek legation so that he might fill both sets of shoes.

A few weeks later they were married. Sarah sent two telegrams to Sardou. The first said, "I am going to die and my greatest regret is not having created your play. Adieu!" The second announced: "I am not dead, I am married." Later she explained about the marriage to her astonished friends, "It's the only thing I haven't experienced." To her son, Sarah began to explain a bit further: "Maurice, *cheri*, I have news for you."

"I know, Maman," the seventeen-year-old broke in coldly, "you have married *Monsieur* Sarah Bernhardt." He did not take kindly to the idea of a permanent rival for his mother's affections. Sarah attempted to divert his attention by buying him a theater. Maurice's venture into the business world was a failure and he ultimately returned to his school studies but not before Sarah had lost many thousands of dollars.

The newlyweds performed in *La Dame aux Camelias* together. Damala left a great deal to be desired in his part, although one critic—the kindest—conceded that "with a great deal of work he might perhaps make a passable actor. Certainly he has with him a great teacher whose coaching should prove profitable."

The same play was then performed in London where the crowd went wild—but only over Sarah. After the last act the future Queen Alexandria came backstage to the Green Room to congratulate the leading lady with: "Oh, Madame, I am so happy to find you alive after the last act!"

Sarcey, the prominent French critic, had braved the English channel to evaluate his favorite on foreign shores. He reported:

Nothing can give an idea of the craze that Sarah Bernhardt is exciting. It's a mania. In the theater where she's about to appear, a tremor runs through the audience; she appears and an "Ah!" of admiration and astonishment escapes from every throat . . . Wherever you go it's her they're discussing.

The only one who wasn't ecstatic was Damala who had begun to regret the impulsive marriage. His jealousy of Sarah brought a secret addiction to morphine out into the open. The marital picture was not improved by Sarah's unqualified success in Sardou's *Fedora*.

After watching Sarah perform in *Fedora,* an admiring Jules Lemaitre wrote:

The electric, chimerical woman has again conquered Paris. Madame Sarah Bernhardt by her characterization, her allure

and her kind of beauty, is eminently a Russian Princess, unless she is a Byzantine Empress or a Begum of Muscat; feline
and impassioned, gentle and violent, innocent and perverse,
neurotic, eccentric, enigmatic, woman-abyss, woman I
known not what. Mme. Sarah Bernhardt always seems like a
strange person returning from far away; she gives me the
feeling of the exotic, and I thank her for reminding me that
the world is wide, and that it cannot be contained in the
shadow of our steeple, and that man is a multiple being, and
capable of everything.

Damala did not share Lemaitre's rapture. An ugly quarrel
followed the opening and Monsieur Sarah Bernhardt departed suddenly for North Africa where he enlisted in an
Algerian regiment. It was a blow to Sarah's pride rather than
to her heart. She, too, had begun to feel an abatement of the
sweet madness that had swept over her in Russia. Many of
Damala's less appealing traits now stood out in bold relief.
Not the least of them was the money that he was costing her.
The man had become an expensive habit.

Bernhardt finished a triumphant run with *Fedora* and then
embarked on a tour of Europe. Traveling with her was a new
love, Jean Richepin. The picture of healthy masculinity, the
man was a surefire antidote to the effete Damala. A former
sharpshooter in the Franco-Prussian War, Richepin had been
in turn a sailor, stevedore, and professional boxer, had lived
with a band of gypsies, and performed as a tumbler-
wrestler-weight-lifter. Added to this, he was an ac-
complished poet, a kind of French Walt Whitman. For Sarah
the man was like a breath of much needed fresh air.

The tour was a financial success as well as a romantic one,
but when Sarah returned home it was to find Damala
stretched out nude on her bed reading a novel. The life of a
legionnaire had proved too rigorous for him and he had returned to the fold.

Confused and embarrassed, Sarah explained to Richepin
that it seemed her duty to try once more with Damala if only
to rescue him from his drug habit. Richepin, for all his ex-
pansive masculinity, accepted life realistically without overdue concern for his ego. Listening sympathetically, with
good humor, he assured Sarah that he understood perfectly,
but added that when she finally threw Damala out of her

home—as he knew she ultimately would—he would be waiting.

And he was. The day came when Sarah simply would not accept Damala's excesses any longer. After pouring her husband's drug supply down the drain, she had him thrown from her house, then obtained a legal separation. Richepin moved in' and proceeded to write two plays, *Nana-Sahib* and *La Glu*, for Sarah and then to adapt *Macbeth* for her. The romance dissolved as the curtain fell on *Macbeth*—not an unqualified success—but the couple remained fast friends for life.

"The family that one has given to one is of no importance," Sarah once said. "The only people who count are those whom one loves and especially the family that one creates oneself." Sarah's lovers always remained in that family.

She was back to touring again—this time to South America. Though critically acclaimed, the run was marred by a serious accident. While leaping to her "death" on stage, Bernhardt somehow missed the mattress hidden behind the set and seriously injured her leg. The limb took a long time to mend and this seems to have been the beginning of the suffering that would plague Sarah for the next thirty years of her life.

Despite the near tragedy, she was able to keep up a rigorous schedule and returned to Paris with enough money to buy a much larger home and a country estate—a 17th century fortress on a tiny island off the coast of Brittany. Both homes were lavishly decorated with *quand meme*—painted on china, engraved on silver, gilded above fireplaces and embroidered on linens.

This was a happy period made more so by another Sarah-Sardou triumph, *La Tosca*. About that time Sarah had an unexpected visit from Prince Henri de Ligne, who asked after their son. It was his first visit in twenty-three years. Upon meeting the young man, Henri settled a generous sum on him and then announced that he wished to legitimatize Maurice, granting him legal permission to bear the proud Belgium name of de Ligne.

Maurice politely refused the name change. Reminding de Ligne that he had been brought up entirely by Sarah, he explained without bitterness that there could be no other name for him but hers. The next day Maurice escorted the departing prince to the railroad station. It was so crowded that day with travelers that special guards had been called to keep order. It was almost departure time and Henri feared that he would miss his train. Approaching a guard, he asked to be allowed through the lines. "I am Prince de Ligne," he said by way of explanation.

"Never heard of you," the guard shrugged. "You'll have to stand in line like all the others." Maurice then interceded. "This gentleman is a relative who must make his train. I am the son of Sarah Bernhardt." An abrupt change came over the officious guard, who suddenly burst into effusive smiles and lead them personally to the platform. As the prince took his seat in the first-class carriage, his son bowed. "You see, sir, the name Bernhardt has its advantages."

Shortly afterward Maurice Bernhardt was married— something few thought would happen for the young man seemed inordinately fond of his mother, who doted on him. A contemporary, Elizabeth Finaly Thomas, in her book of memoirs, *Ladies, Lovers and Other People*, described the mother of the groom thusly:

> We were barely seated when a murmur swept the church: "Voici Sarah!" A slender figure scarcely more tangible than a column of smoke was floating up the aisle. A cloak of grey velvet opened over a skirt of soft pink faille. The white heart-shaped face, blurred at the edges by the marabou of her coat, and the fluffy masses of her extraordinary blond hair were crowned by the misty tulle of her bonnet. Over her large white teeth, her reddened lips drew back in that smile of conscious fascination which is part of the daily toilette of every Frenchwoman. As she passed us on the arm of her escort, I heard for the first time the golden voice made famous by the critics. The adoration of her son, by this woman of many loves and lovers, was well known.

Maurice's wife was a Polish princess, Terka Jabonowska, whose feelings at being upstaged at her own wedding were not recorded. Unfortunately this was only the first instance. Sarah had extracted the promise that Maurice would visit her once a day. He more than kept his word, dropping by two and even three times in a single day. Only Sarah's tours separated them. If Terka imagined that her day would come, it didn't—in this lifetime anyway. Sarah was to outlive her daughter-in-law by many years.

In 1889 Sarah received word that her thirty-four-year-old husband, Jacques Damala, was dying. Hurrying directly to his shabby room, she found a totally broken man. Impulsively Sarah arranged to have Damala moved to her own home where she hired round-the-clock medical care and even nursed him herself. She was at his side when he died a few weeks later. Sarah then arranged to have his body shipped home to Greece along with a bust that she had made of him to be placed upon his tomb. Whenever her tours took her to Athens, Sarah invariably made a pilgrimage to Damala's grave.

Now at forty-five, Sarah was not only a widow but a grandmother. The latter fact she shared eagerly with the world at large; she was delighted with the baby, Simone. Bernhardt still retained her trim figure and youthful face. Dramatic proof of this was offered when she appeared as the nineteen-year-old *Jeanne d'Arc*. The reviews were glowing. She was to repeat this triumph many times in the years to come.

Once again Sarah saw evidence of the anti-Semitism that smoldered just below the surface in late 19th century Europe. The Dreyfus case exploded upon the French with ugly repercussions that would not die until the first World War. A young officer of Jewish descent had been accused of treason and exiled to Devil's Island. Sarah witnessed the man's public degradation, the breaking of his sword, the ripping off of his insignia and medals. Instinctively she sensed his innocence and had spoken out against the inconclusiveness of the proof that had convicted him. It is difficult after nearly eighty years to understand the blind hate that seemed to envelop the entire country, defying all reason and setting brother against brother, family against family, yet this is what happened. Careers were broken, romances severed, fortunes made and fortunes lost depending solely upon how one viewed the Dreyfus case.

So violent were the hostilities aroused that when evidence was uncovered that actually indicated Dreyfus's innocence, it was suppressed by the army who then branded those who had uncovered it as traitors. Sarah, confident that Dreyfus was not guilty, felt that only one man was capable of rousing the sleeping conscience of the country to the injustice of the punishment. She went herself to Emile Zola and persuaded the famous writer to lend his support to the "Dreyfusards." Convinced by her entreaty, Zola wrote the highly inflammatory *J'Accuse!* thereby mobilizing Dreyfus' defense.

The next day headlines read, "Sarah Bernhardt has joined the Jews against the army." All of Paris recamped into pro-Sarah factions and anti-Sarah factions. Tragically Maurice was among the latter. He quarreled angrily with the mother he adored and moved with his wife and small daughters to southern France.

Much of the ensuing bitterness ended in 1896 when Sarah was given a "Day of Glorification," a tribute organized by the most renowned writers in France—a group that had previously been divided by the Dreyfus issue. It was a dramatic occasion attended by five hundred of the capitol's arbiters of fashion and culture. There was hardly a dry eye present as tribute after tribute was heaped upon the courageous woman.. Maurice having only recently reconciled with her was overcome with emotion. "Nobody knows my mother," he sobbed. "She's good, a gallant woman."

In 1899 Bernhardt decided to open a theater of her own. The Theatre des Nations in the Place du Chatelet was available and she preceded to sign a twenty-five-year lease. She was now fifty-five. Her first move upon acquiring the theater was to rename the place the Theatre Sarah Bernhardt, a name it retained until the Nazi occupation in World War II. (When it was learned that Sarah was half Jewish the Nazis changed it back to the original.) From 1899 to 1915, Sarah was to appear there in forty different roles, twenty-five of them new creations. One of the most delightful was *The Sleeping Beauty* adapted by her old friend and former lover, Richepin. In this fairy tale she appeared as Prince Charming. She was sixty-three.

At sixty-five, Sarah again played the part of *Jeanne d'Arc*. The opening night audience came prepared to laugh but stayed to cheer. Somehow Sarah seemed to embody the naive, innocent girl. At one moment during the tribunal scene she was questioned by her interrogator. "What is your name?" the Grand Inquisitor asked as her heavy iron fetters were removed.

"Jeanne."

"What is your age?"

Quietly, turning to face the audience directly, Sarah spoke the word clearly. "Nineteen."

The audience seemed to gasp as one, not with incredulity as one might expect, but rather in wonder and admiration. Sarah *was* nineteen. Then came a thunder of applause. It seemed that a second Jeanne had performed a miracle as great as the first.

At about the same time a friend asked Sarah when she intended to give up love. "With my dying breath," was her answer. "I intend to live as I have always lived." In 1910 she took off on her second "Farewell American Tour." This time the leading man and resident lover was Lou Tellegen, a young man so handsome that he had recently served as the model for Rodin's statue Eternal Springtime. During their four year partnership the two were inseparable. Tellegen played Lord Essex to Sarah's Queen Elizabeth in a silent film produced by Adolph Zukor in 1912. The following year he accompanied her on a third farewell tour, remaining behind in New York when she returned to Paris.

"I would have been a much happier man had I remained with her until the end of her career," Tellegen wrote later. "Every moment that I worked with her, I knew the best the theater can give and, remembering the most glorious four years of my life, my eyes fill with tears and my heart cries out, 'Madame! Grande Madame! I am so alone without you!'"

On March 16, 1914, Sarah was made a Chevalier of the Legion d'Honneur. For once she was speechless and stood sobbing before the cheering crowd, most of whom were crying too.

The following summer brought the onslaught of World War I. In a grim repeat of a previous drama, Sarah's friends begged her to leave Paris and again she refused to do so. When it was discovered by the Ministry of War that Sarah Bernhardt's name had been placed by the Kaiser on a list of most wanted hostages, Georges Clemenceau—soon to be Prime Minister of France—was dispatched to insist that she leave. Understandably flattered, Sarah complied in the interests of France—if not her own. She was a few months short of her seventieth birthday.

Chronic pain in her right knee was now causing so much trouble that it was necessary to keep the whole leg immobile in a plaster cast. As months passed and the pain grew worse, a physician was summoned from Paris to examine her. Apprehensive at the thought of performing radical surgery upon a woman her age with a history of uremic poisoning, the doctor asked, "It's gangrene, what shall I do?"

She shrugged in resignation, "Since there is nothing else to be done, why ask my opinion?" Her right leg was removed almost to the hip. For a time the actress' life hung in the balance while the whole world waited. Then slowly her strength began to return.

A wooden leg had been fashioned specially for her but the only means of fastening it was by a heavy girdle that fit about her hips and stomach. She had never worn a corset and wasn't about to begin at seventy-one. Angrily she ordered the artificial leg thrown into the fire. The idea of a wheelchair was also rejected. "I'm not some old invalid," she fumed. The only solution left for one who had never even considered giving up was a litter. This means of conveyance was painted white at Sarah's instruction and finished in Louis XV style with gilt carving.

Elizabeth Finlay Thomas saw her carried through the stage door one evening and wrote, "Her arms full of roses, the shining fuzz of her hair crowned with her usual capote of flowers, her mutilated figure a mass of velvets, she was the personification of undaunted courage."

Eight months after her surgery, Sarah was back onstage again. She produced three one-act plays and appeared herself in the third. In this, Sarah spoke her lines while sitting on a dais, but ended by somehow rising on one leg and continuing to recite her lines for a time balanced in this way. How she performed this superhuman feat no one knew but the effect upon the audience was electrifying.

The war dragged on and Sarah continued to perform at the front. Once her companion was the young comedienne, Beatrix Dussanne, who wrote how Sarah became remarkably adept at hopping about on one leg and laughing at her own condition. She described Sarah as "an old woman heroically and insanely determined to ignore time, pain and physical laws, smiling and joking to forestall being pitied, shedding on the public the warmth of a radiance that never goes out. Greater perhaps in this glowing twilight than in the sparkling days of her apogee."

There was one more "farewell" tour to the United States—this one truly the last—which continued for eighteen months. It was a triumph of endurance as well as acting skill. The bill consisted of scenes from her regular repertory as well as two new one-act plays by Maurice and one of her own.

During this tour, Sarah was rushed to Mt. Sinai Hospital for emergency surgery. An infected kidney was removed. "They can cut out everything as long as they leave my head," she quipped. During her convalescence, Sarah kept busy reading plays, writing short stories and designing clothes. In an interview given at this time, she scoffed at any idea of resting on her laurels. "My ideal? My ideal—but I am still pursuing it. I shall pursue it until my last hour, and I feel that in the supreme moment I shall know the certainty of attaining it beyond the tomb."

The tour was resumed with only a short interruption of the schedule.

Back in Paris she opened in *Daniel,* a romantic play written especially for her. Sarah, who had in the past played Prince Charming, Hamlet and Peleas, appeared as a man—one of two brothers in love with the same woman. Daniel, the loser, had taken to drugs and become a semi-invalid and yet it is he who shaped the play. It was a highly romantic part and Sarah, at seventy-six, carried it off well.

The play then went on tour and Sarah with it. In Madrid, men took off their jackets to place on the street for her litter bearers to walk upon. In London, Sarah replied to Queen Mary who had asked how she could bear up under the strain of performing every day, "I shall die on the stage; it is my battlefield." Later on the same tour, Sarah confided to a friend, "You remember my motto, *Quand meme?* In case of necessity, I shall have myself strapped to the scenery."

In autumn of 1922, Sarah began rehearsing *Un Sujet de Roman.* She adored her part and was looking forward to opening night with great anticipation. Then on the night of the dress rehearsal she collapsed into a coma that lasted an hour. Sarah's first words upon reviving were "When do I go on?"

The answer was "never" but fortunately she did not know it then.

The play went on without Sarah but she continued to rehearse her lines, certain that she would one day perform the part. While convalescing from the uremic attack, she was asked to do the part of a clairvoyant in a movie called *LaVoyante.* Since the actress was too ill to go to the studio, it came to her instead. Scenery, klieg lights, and cameras were all installed in Sarah's drawing room and the work began.

"They're paying me 10,000 francs a day," she confided to a caller. "It's as good as going to America. I wonder when my next tour will be."

It was on this characteristic note of optimism and expectation that Sarah collapsed from another attack of uremia and was returned to bed for the last time. "All my life reporters have tormented me enough. I can tease them now a little by making them cool their heels," she smiled with a touch of mischief. Those were her last words. The following day Sarah Bernhardt was dead at seventy-eight.

Thirty thousand mourners passed by the rosewood coffin—the same one she'd kept in readiness for nearly sixty years. There were millions of flowers and nearly as many printed eulogies.

Among them was that of the critic Maurice Baring, who prophesied: "When in the future people will say, 'But you should have seen Sarah Bernhardt in the part,' the newcomers will probably shrug their shoulders and say, 'Oh, we have heard such things before.' But they will not know, nor will anybody be able to tell them, or explain to them, what Sarah Bernhardt could do with a modulated inflection, a look, a gesture, a cry, a smile, a sigh . . ."

But possibly the most appropriate words ever written about Sarah Bernhardt were those of Lamaitre:

> Perhaps you have not been one of the most reasonable women of this century, but you will have lived more than multitudes of others and you will have been one of the most gracious of apparitions that ever soared for the consolation of man across the changing face of this world of phenomena.

Bibliography

Victoria Woodhull

Douglas, Emily Taft. *Remember the Ladies,* G.P. Putnam's Sons, 1966.
Holbrook, Stewart H. *Dreamers of the American Dream,* Doubleday, 1957.
Johnson, Gerald W. *The Lunatic Fringe,* Lippincott, 1957.
Johnson, Johanna. *Mrs. Satan,* G.P. Putnam's Sons, 1967.
Marberry, M.M. *Vicky,* Funk & Wagnalls, 1967.
Pearson, Hesketh. *The Marrying Americans,* Coward McCann, 1961.
Ross, Ishbell. *Charmers and Cranks,* Harper & Row, 1965.
_____. *Ladies of the Press,* Harper and Brothers, 1936.
Shaplen, Robert. *Free Love and Heavenly Sinners,* Knopf, 1954.
Stern, Madeleine B. *We the Women,* Schulte,1963.
Wallace, Irving. *The Nympho and Other Maniacs,* Simon and Schuster, 1971.
_____. *The Square Pegs,* Knopf, 1957.

Amelia Earhart

Balchen, Bernt. *Come North With Me,* Dutton, 1958.
Briand, Paul L. Jr. *Daughter of the Sky,* Duell, Sloan and Pearce, 1960.
Burke, John. *Winged Legend,* Putnam, 1970.
Cochran, Jacqueline. *The Stars at Noon,* Little, Brown and Company, 1954.
Earhart, Amelia. *The Fun of It,* Brewer, Warren & Putnam, 1932.
_____. *Last Flight,* (Geo. P. Putnam, ed.) Putnam, 1937.
Goerner, Fred. *The Search for Amelia Earhart,* Doubleday, 1966.
Klaas, Joe. *Amelia Earhart Lives,* McGraw-Hill, 1970.
Morrissey, Muriel Earhart. *Courage is the Price,* McCormick-Armstrong, 1963.
Nichols, Ruth. *Wings for Life,* Lippincott, 1957.
Stripple, Dick. *Amelia Earhart: The Myth and Reality,* Exposition, 1972.
Thaden, Louise. *High, Wide and Frightened,* Stackpole Sons, 1938.

Isadora Duncan

Desti, Mary. *The Untold Story,* H. Liveright, 1929.
Duncan, Isadora. *My Life,* Liveright Pub., 1927.
Duncan, Irma. *Duncan Dancer,* Wesleyan University Press, 1966.
MacDougall, Allan Ross. *Isadora, a Revolutionary in Art and Love,* Thomas Nelson & Sons, 1960.
Richey, Elinor. *Eminent Women of the West,* Howell North, 1975.
Ross, Ishbel. *Charmers and Cranks,* Harper & Row, 1965.
Schneider, Ilya Ilyich. *Isadora Duncan, the Russian Years,* Harcourt, Brace & World, 1968.
Seroff, Victor. *The Real Isadora,* Dial Press, 1971.
Steegmuller, Francis, ed. *Your Isadora: the Love Story of Isadora Duncan and Gordon Craig,* Random House, 1974.
Wagenknecht, Edward Charles. *Seven Daughters of the Theater,* University of Oklahoma Press, 1964.

Helena Blavatsky

Allen, Jane. "The Feminine Mystique of Madame Blavatsky" *Borderline Magazine*, November 1964.

Blavatsky, H.P. *Isis Unveiled, a Master-Key to the Mysteries of Ancient and Modern Science and Theology*, Aryan Theosophical Press, Revised Third Point Loma Edition, 1919.

_____. *Blavatksy Collected Writings, 1874–1878*, Theosophical Press, 1966.

_____. *Dynamics of the Psychic World*, The Theosophical Publishing House, 1972.

Endersby, Victor A. *The Hall of Magic Mirrors, a Portrait of Madame Blavatsky*, Carlton Press, 1969.

Hower, Virginia. *H.P. Blavatsky and the Secret Doctrine*, Edited by Virginia Hower, The Theosophical Publishing House, Wheaton, Ill., 1971.

Neff, Mary K. *Personal Memoirs of H.P. Blavatsky*, Dutton, 1937.

Olcott, Henry Steel. *Inside the Occult, The True Story of Madame Blavatsky*, Running Press, 1975.

_____. *The Key to Theosophy*, The Theosophical Publishing House, original complete edition 1889; abridged Quest edition 1972.

Symonds, John. *The Lady With the Magic Eyes*, Thomas Yoseloff, 1959.

Vonnegut, Kurt Jr. "The Mysterious Madame Blavatsky," *McCalls'*, March 1970.

Williams, Gertrude Marvin. *Priestess of the Occult*, Knopf, 1946.

Ernestine Schumann-Heink

Huff, Warren and Edna Lenore,. editors, *Famous Americans,* Charles Webb, 1941.

Klein, Herman. *Great Women Singers of My Time*, Dutton, 1931.

Lawton, Mary. *Schumann-Heink, the Last of the Titans*, Macmillan, 1928.

Palmer, Opal Y. "Madame Schumann-Heink," *The Rosicrucian Digest*, July, 1975.

Wagner, Alan. *Prima Donnas and Other Wild Beasts*, Argonaut Books, 1961.

Sarah Bernhardt

Baring, Maurice. *Sarah Bernhardt*, Appleton-Century, 1934.

Bernhardt, Sarah. *Memories of My Life*, Appleton and Co., 1907.

Bradford, Gamaliel. *Daughters of Eve*, Houghton Mifflin, 1930.

Emboden, William. *Sarah Bernhardt*, Macmillan, 1975.

Skinner, Cornelia Otis. *Madame Sarah*, Houghton Mifflin, 1967.

Tellegen, Lou. *Women Have Been Kind*, Vanguard Press, 1931.

Thomas, Elizabeth Finley. *Ladies, Lovers and Other People*, Longmans Green, 1935.

Verneuil, Louis. *The Fabulous Life of Sarah Bernhardt*, Harper & Row, 1942.

Wagenknecht, Edward. *Seven Daughters of the Theater*, University of Oklahoma Press, 1964.

INDEX